CHINESE NAMES, SURN
LOCATIONS & ADDRE

中国大陆地址集

GUANGXI ZHUANG AUTONOMOUS REGION - PART 1

广西壮族自治区

ZIYUE TANG

汤子玥

ACKNOWLEDGEMENT

I am deeply indebted to my friends and family members to support me throughout my life. Without their invaluable love and guidance, this work wouldn't have been possible.

Thank you

Ziyue Tang

汤子玥

PREFACE

The book introduces foreigner students to the Chinese names along with locations and addresses from the **Guangxi Zhuang Autonomous Region** of China (中国广西壮族自治区). The book contains 150 entries (names, addresses) explained with simplified Chinese characters, pinyin and English.

Chinese names follow the standard convention where the given name is written after the surname. For example, in 王威 (Wang Wei), Wang is the surname, and Wei is the given name. Further, the surnames are generally made of one (王) or two characters (司马). Similarly, the given names are also made of either one or two characters. For example, 司马威 (Sima Wei) is a three character Chinese name suitable for men. 司马威威 is a four character Chinese name.

Chinese addresses are comprised of different administrative units that start with the largest geographic entity (country) and continue to the smallest entity (county, building names, room number). For example, a typical address in Nanjing city (capital of Jiangsu province) would look like 江苏省南京市清华路 28 栋 520 室 (Jiāngsū shěng nánjīng shì qīnghuá lù 28 dòng 520 shì; Room 520, Building 28, Qinghua Road, Nanjing City, Jiangsu Province).

CONTENTS

ACKNOWLEDGEMENT 2

PREFACE 3

CONTENTS 4

CHAPTER 1: NAME, SURNAME & ADDRESSES (1-30) 5

CHAPTER 2: NAME, SURNAME & ADDRESSES (31-60) 17

CHAPTER 3: NAME, SURNAME & ADDRESSES (61-90) 29

CHAPTER 4: NAME, SURNAME & ADDRESSES (91-120) 41

CHAPTER 5: NAME, SURNAME & ADDRESSES (121-150) 53

CHAPTER 1: NAME, SURNAME & ADDRESSES (1-30)

1。姓名: 商可阳

住址（公共汽车站）：广西壮族自治区河池市南丹县帆仲路 475 号茂泽站（邮政编码：598595）。联系电话：72861628。电子邮箱：cwtia@nmhrxtfz.transport.cn

Zhù zhǐ: Shāng Kě Yáng Guǎngxī Zhuàngzú Zìzhìqū Héchí Shì Nán Dān Xiàn Fān Zhòng Lù 475 Hào Mào Zé Zhàn (Yóuzhèng Biānmǎ：598595). Liánxì Diànhuà：72861628. Diànzǐ Yóuxiāng：cwtia@nmhrxtfz.transport.cn

Ke Yang Shang, Mao Ze Bus Station, 475 Fan Zhong Road, Nandan County, Hechi, Guangxi Autonomous Region. Postal Code: 598595. Phone Number：72861628. E-mail：cwtia@nmhrxtfz.transport.cn

2。姓名: 强浩渊

住址（寺庙）：广西壮族自治区南宁市邕宁区兆继路 358 号自秀寺（邮政编码：564743）。联系电话：42819584。电子邮箱：uhywi@fndclzaw.god.cn

Zhù zhǐ: Qiáng Hào Yuān Guǎngxī Zhuàngzú Zìzhìqū Nánníng Shì Yōng Níng Qū Zhào Jì Lù 358 Hào Zì Xiù Sì (Yóuzhèng Biānmǎ：564743). Liánxì Diànhuà：42819584. Diànzǐ Yóuxiāng：uhywi@fndclzaw.god.cn

Hao Yuan Qiang, Zi Xiu Temple, 358 Zhao Ji Road, Yongning District, NanNing, Guangxi Autonomous Region. Postal Code: 564743. Phone Number：42819584. E-mail：uhywi@fndclzaw.god.cn

3。姓名: 海茂焯

住址（公司）：广西壮族自治区柳州市柳江区波易路 178 号秀队有限公司（邮政编码：517528）。联系电话：21527910。电子邮箱：bkesq@wytgxijz.biz.cn

Zhù zhǐ: Hǎi Mào Zhuō Guǎngxī Zhuàngzú Zìzhìqū Liǔzhōu Shì Liǔjiāng Qū Bō Yì Lù 178 Hào Xiù Duì Yǒuxiàn Gōngsī (Yóuzhèng Biānmǎ：517528). Liánxì Diànhuà：21527910. Diànzǐ Yóuxiāng：bkesq@wytgxijz.biz.cn

Mao Zhuo Hai, Xiu Dui Corporation, 178 Bo Yi Road, Liujiang District, Liuzhou, Guangxi Autonomous Region. Postal Code: 517528. Phone Number：21527910. E-mail：bkesq@wytgxijz.biz.cn

4。姓名: 方辉帆

住址（火车站）：广西壮族自治区玉林市福绵区稼陶路 229 号玉林站（邮政编码：342088）。联系电话：27866845。电子邮箱：psqxk@emnxhjqy.chr.cn

Zhù zhǐ: Fāng Huī Fān Guǎngxī Zhuàngzú Zìzhìqū Yùlín Shì Fú Mián Qū Jià Táo Lù 229 Hào Yùlín Zhàn (Yóuzhèng Biānmǎ：342088). Liánxì Diànhuà：27866845. Diànzǐ Yóuxiāng：psqxk@emnxhjqy.chr.cn

Hui Fan Fang, Yulin Railway Station, 229 Jia Tao Road, Fumian District, Yulin, Guangxi Autonomous Region. Postal Code: 342088. Phone Number：27866845. E-mail：psqxk@emnxhjqy.chr.cn

5。姓名: 荣盛懂

住址（博物院）：广西壮族自治区崇左市凭祥市坡守路 625 号崇左博物馆（邮政编码：858683）。联系电话：33268613。电子邮箱：thpqo@zgwamcbv.museums.cn

Zhù zhǐ: Róng Chéng Dǒng Guǎngxī Zhuàngzú Zìzhìqū Chóng Zuǒ Shì Píng xiáng shì Pō Shǒu Lù 625 Hào Cóng Zuǒ Bó Wù Guǎn (Yóuzhèng Biānmǎ：858683). Liánxì Diànhuà：33268613. Diànzǐ Yóuxiāng：thpqo@zgwamcbv.museums.cn

Cheng Dong Rong, Chongzuo Museum, 625 Po Shou Road, Pingxiang City, Chongzuo, Guangxi Autonomous Region. Postal Code: 858683. Phone Number：33268613. E-mail：thpqo@zgwamcbv.museums.cn

6。姓名: 丰伦斌

住址（寺庙）：广西壮族自治区崇左市宁明县人王路 232 号原盛寺（邮政编码：914479）。联系电话：97005758。电子邮箱：cviqj@hyuoxbsg.god.cn

Zhù zhǐ: Fēng Lún Bīn Guǎngxī Zhuàngzú Zìzhìqū Chóng Zuǒ Shì Níng Míng Xiàn Rén Wàng Lù 232 Hào Yuán Shèng Sì (Yóuzhèng Biānmǎ：914479). Liánxì Diànhuà：97005758. Diànzǐ Yóuxiāng：cviqj@hyuoxbsg.god.cn

Lun Bin Feng, Yuan Sheng Temple, 232 Ren Wang Road, Ningming County, Chongzuo, Guangxi Autonomous Region. Postal Code: 914479. Phone Number：97005758. E-mail：cviqj@hyuoxbsg.god.cn

7。姓名: 荣民坤

住址（湖泊）：广西壮族自治区桂林市七星区龙中路 357 号骥食湖（邮政编码：151895）。联系电话：11333262。电子邮箱：phwmy@xlcbnaiv.lakes.cn

Zhù zhǐ: Róng Mín Kūn Guǎngxī Zhuàngzú Zìzhìqū Guìlín Shì Qīxīng Qū Lóng Zhòng Lù 357 Hào Jì Shí Hú (Yóuzhèng Biānmǎ：151895). Liánxì Diànhuà：11333262. Diànzǐ Yóuxiāng：phwmy@xlcbnaiv.lakes.cn

Min Kun Rong, Ji Shi Lake, 357 Long Zhong Road, Qixing District, Guilin, Guangxi Autonomous Region. Postal Code: 151895. Phone Number：11333262. E-mail：phwmy@xlcbnaiv.lakes.cn

8。姓名: 晏翰队

住址（火车站）：广西壮族自治区梧州市岑溪市福石路 550 号梧州站（邮政编码：713146）。联系电话：35929146。电子邮箱：incyx@itflkayh.chr.cn

Zhù zhǐ: Yàn Hàn Duì Guǎngxī Zhuàngzú Zìzhìqū Wúzhōu Shì Cénxī Shì Fú Shí Lù 550 Hào Wúzōu Zhàn (Yóuzhèng Biānmǎ：713146). Liánxì Diànhuà：35929146. Diànzǐ Yóuxiāng：incyx@itflkayh.chr.cn

Han Dui Yan, Wuzhou Railway Station, 550 Fu Shi Road, Cenxi City, Wuzhou, Guangxi Autonomous Region. Postal Code: 713146. Phone Number：35929146. E-mail：incyx@itflkayh.chr.cn

9。姓名: 丰轼冕

住址（医院）：广西壮族自治区北海市银海区土振路 138 号队德医院（邮政编码：275214）。联系电话：88622016。电子邮箱：yurjt@konpvymq.health.cn

Zhù zhǐ: Fēng Shì Miǎn Guǎngxī Zhuàngzú Zìzhìqū Běihǎi Shì Yín Hǎi Qū Tǔ Zhèn Lù 138 Hào Duì Dé Yī Yuàn (Yóuzhèng Biānmǎ：275214). Liánxì Diànhuà：88622016. Diànzǐ Yóuxiāng：yurjt@konpvymq.health.cn

Shi Mian Feng, Dui De Hospital, 138 Tu Zhen Road, Yinhai District, Beihai, Guangxi Autonomous Region. Postal Code: 275214. Phone Number：88622016. E-mail：yurjt@konpvymq.health.cn

10。姓名: 龚乙威

住址（家庭）：广西壮族自治区玉林市陆川县石强路 282 号冕全公寓 16 层 529 室（邮政编码：434360）。联系电话：71620849。电子邮箱：ljksu@wzhpdlyu.cn

Zhù zhǐ: Gōng Yǐ Wēi Guǎngxī Zhuàngzú Zìzhìqū Yùlín Shì Lù Chuān Xiàn Dàn Qiáng Lù 282 Hào Miǎn Quán Gōng Yù 16 Céng 529 Shì (Yóuzhèng Biānmǎ：434360). Liánxì Diànhuà：71620849. Diànzǐ Yóuxiāng：ljksu@wzhpdlyu.cn

Yi Wei Gong, Room# 529, Floor# 16, Mian Quan Apartment, 282 Dan Qiang Road, Luchuan County, Yulin, Guangxi Autonomous Region. Postal Code: 434360. Phone Number：71620849. E-mail：ljksu@wzhpdlyu.cn

11。姓名: 宗阳鹤

住址（公司）：广西壮族自治区来宾市金秀瑶族自治县屹盛路 429 号仓盛有限公司（邮政编码：781019）。联系电话：90751857。电子邮箱：nhtpu@fhkdanjy.biz.cn

Zhù zhǐ: Zōng Yáng Hè Guǎngxī Zhuàngzú Zìzhìqū Láibīn Shì Jīn Xiù Yáozú Zìzhìxiàn Yì Shèng Lù 429 Hào Cāng Chéng Yǒuxiàn Gōngsī (Yóuzhèng Biānmǎ: 781019). Liánxì Diànhuà: 90751857. Diànzǐ Yóuxiāng: nhtpu@fhkdanjy.biz.cn

Yang He Zong, Cang Cheng Corporation, 429 Yi Sheng Road, Jinxiu Yao Autonomous County, Laibin, Guangxi Autonomous Region. Postal Code: 781019. Phone Number: 90751857. E-mail: nhtpu@fhkdanjy.biz.cn

12。姓名: 凤毅辙

住址（寺庙）：广西壮族自治区柳州市城中区王淹路 300 号翰计寺（邮政编码：662025）。联系电话：55568397。电子邮箱：rckwx@zrawyiud.god.cn

Zhù zhǐ: Fèng Yì Zhé Guǎngxī Zhuàngzú Zìzhìqū Liǔzhōu Shì Chéngzhōng Qū Wáng Yān Lù 300 Hào Hàn Jì Sì (Yóuzhèng Biānmǎ: 662025). Liánxì Diànhuà: 55568397. Diànzǐ Yóuxiāng: rckwx@zrawyiud.god.cn

Yi Zhe Feng, Han Ji Temple, 300 Wang Yan Road, Chengzhong District, Liuzhou, Guangxi Autonomous Region. Postal Code: 662025. Phone Number: 55568397. E-mail: rckwx@zrawyiud.god.cn

13。姓名: 井员启

住址（家庭）：广西壮族自治区河池市南丹县九洵路 348 号游山公寓 30 层 429 室（邮政编码：225927）。联系电话：89763429。电子邮箱：qxnyc@uzhyqcsm.cn

Zhù zhǐ: Jǐng Yún Qǐ Guǎngxī Zhuàngzú Zìzhìqū Héchí Shì Nán Dān Xiàn Jiǔ Xún Lù 348 Hào Yóu Shān Gōng Yù 30 Céng 429 Shì (Yóuzhèng Biānmǎ: 225927). Liánxì Diànhuà: 89763429. Diànzǐ Yóuxiāng: qxnyc@uzhyqcsm.cn

Yun Qi Jing, Room# 429, Floor# 30, You Shan Apartment, 348 Jiu Xun Road, Nandan County, Hechi, Guangxi Autonomous Region. Postal Code: 225927. Phone Number: 89763429. E-mail: qxnyc@uzhyqcsm.cn

14。姓名: 黄豪俊

住址（大学）：广西壮族自治区河池市南丹县强德大学冠谢路 978 号（邮政编码：456036）。联系电话：78156024。电子邮箱：xsvpm@xkbaplot.edu.cn

Zhù zhǐ: Huáng Háo Jùn Guǎngxī Zhuàngzú Zìzhìqū Héchí Shì Nán Dān Xiàn Qiáng Dé DàxuéGuàn Xiè Lù 978 Hào（Yóuzhèng Biānmǎ：456036). Liánxì Diànhuà：78156024. Diànzǐ Yóuxiāng：xsvpm@xkbaplot.edu.cn

Hao Jun Huang, Qiang De University, 978 Guan Xie Road, Nandan County, Hechi, Guangxi Autonomous Region. Postal Code: 456036. Phone Number：78156024. E-mail：xsvpm@xkbaplot.edu.cn

15。姓名: 傅石沛

住址（寺庙）：广西壮族自治区柳州市柳江区先葛路 760 号土汉寺（邮政编码：498511）。联系电话：57202759。电子邮箱：jtirw@lqbkemix.god.cn

Zhù zhǐ: Fù Shí Bèi Guǎngxī Zhuàngzú Zìzhìqū Liǔzhōu Shì Liǔjiāng Qū Xiān Gé Lù 760 Hào Tǔ Hàn Sì（Yóuzhèng Biānmǎ：498511). Liánxì Diànhuà：57202759. Diànzǐ Yóuxiāng：jtirw@lqbkemix.god.cn

Shi Bei Fu, Tu Han Temple, 760 Xian Ge Road, Liujiang District, Liuzhou, Guangxi Autonomous Region. Postal Code: 498511. Phone Number：57202759. E-mail：jtirw@lqbkemix.god.cn

16。姓名: 索南圣

住址（医院）：广西壮族自治区河池市环江毛南族自治县队南路 799 号国学医院（邮政编码：120894）。联系电话：57767250。电子邮箱：txnsj@kvebarhf.health.cn

Zhù zhǐ: Suǒ Nán Shèng Guǎngxī Zhuàngzú Zìzhìqū Héchí Shì Huán Jiāng Máonán Zú Zìzhìxiàn Duì Nán Lù 799 Hào Guó Xué Yī Yuàn（Yóuzhèng Biānmǎ：120894). Liánxì Diànhuà：57767250. Diànzǐ Yóuxiāng：txnsj@kvebarhf.health.cn

Nan Sheng Suo, Guo Xue Hospital, 799 Dui Nan Road, Huanjiang Maonan Autonomous County, Hechi, Guangxi Autonomous Region. Postal Code: 120894. Phone Number：57767250. E-mail：txnsj@kvebarhf.health.cn

17。姓名: 路南强

住址（公共汽车站）：广西壮族自治区梧州市藤县翰葛路 229 号奎坤站（邮政编码：712032）。联系电话：73552374。电子邮箱：yihwf@eldncrua.transport.cn

Zhù zhǐ: Lù Nán Qiǎng Guǎngxī Zhuàngzú Zìzhìqū Wúzhōu Shì Téng Xiàn Hàn Gé Lù 229 Hào Kuí Kūn Zhàn（Yóuzhèng Biānmǎ：712032). Liánxì Diànhuà：73552374. Diànzǐ Yóuxiāng：yihwf@eldncrua.transport.cn

Nan Qiang Lu, Kui Kun Bus Station, 229 Han Ge Road, Fuji County, Wuzhou, Guangxi Autonomous Region. Postal Code: 712032. Phone Number：73552374. E-mail：yihwf@eldncrua.transport.cn

18。姓名: 周队斌

住址（公共汽车站）：广西壮族自治区钦州市钦北区舟岐路 238 号水泽站（邮政编码：298888）。联系电话：20256483。电子邮箱：udzyj@yksaxjot.transport.cn

Zhù zhǐ: Zhōu Duì Bīn Guǎngxī Zhuàngzú Zìzhìqū Qīnzhōu Shì Qīn Běi Qū Zhōu Qí Lù 238 Hào Shuǐ Zé Zhàn（Yóuzhèng Biānmǎ：298888). Liánxì Diànhuà：20256483. Diànzǐ Yóuxiāng：udzyj@yksaxjot.transport.cn

Dui Bin Zhou, Shui Ze Bus Station, 238 Zhou Qi Road, Qinbei District, Qinzhou, Guangxi Autonomous Region. Postal Code: 298888. Phone Number：20256483. E-mail：udzyj@yksaxjot.transport.cn

19。姓名: 阚兵独

住址（机场）：广西壮族自治区钦州市钦北区其大路 119 号钦州土龙国际机场（邮政编码：497422）。联系电话：70673750。电子邮箱：hszmc@kbzocnhx.airports.cn

Zhù zhǐ: Kàn Bīng Dú Guǎngxī Zhuàngzú Zìzhìqū Qīnzhōu Shì Qīn Běi Qū Qí Dà Lù 119 Hào Qīnzōu Tǔ Lóng Guó Jì Jī Chǎng（Yóuzhèng Biānmǎ：497422）. Liánxì Diànhuà：70673750. Diànzǐ Yóuxiāng：hszmc@kbzocnhx.airports.cn

Bing Du Kan, Qinzhou Tu Long International Airport, 119 Qi Da Road, Qinbei District, Qinzhou, Guangxi Autonomous Region. Postal Code: 497422. Phone Number：70673750. E-mail：hszmc@kbzocnhx.airports.cn

20。姓名: 韩际南

住址（公司）：广西壮族自治区崇左市江州区独征路 190 号葛易有限公司（邮政编码：894276）。联系电话：31907788。电子邮箱：zofds@ejvzkhts.biz.cn

Zhù zhǐ: Hán Jì Nán Guǎngxī Zhuàngzú Zìzhìqū Chóng Zuǒ Shì Jiāng Zhōu Qū Dú Zhēng Lù 190 Hào Gé Yì Yǒuxiàn Gōngsī（Yóuzhèng Biānmǎ：894276）. Liánxì Diànhuà：31907788. Diànzǐ Yóuxiāng：zofds@ejvzkhts.biz.cn

Ji Nan Han, Ge Yi Corporation, 190 Du Zheng Road, Jiangzhou District, Chongzuo, Guangxi Autonomous Region. Postal Code: 894276. Phone Number：31907788. E-mail：zofds@ejvzkhts.biz.cn

21。姓名: 侯圣超

住址（公司）：广西壮族自治区河池市大化瑶族自治县智仓路 858 号山继有限公司（邮政编码：250416）。联系电话：21019329。电子邮箱：zdycf@pqcvlyfa.biz.cn

Zhù zhǐ: Hóu Shèng Chāo Guǎngxī Zhuàngzú Zìzhìqū Héchí Shì Dà Huà Yáozú Zìzhìxiàn Zhì Cāng Lù 858 Hào Shān Jì Yǒuxiàn Gōngsī（Yóuzhèng Biānmǎ：250416）. Liánxì Diànhuà：21019329. Diànzǐ Yóuxiāng：zdycf@pqcvlyfa.biz.cn

Sheng Chao Hou, Shan Ji Corporation, 858 Zhi Cang Road, Dahua Yao Autonomous County, Hechi, Guangxi Autonomous Region. Postal Code: 250416. Phone Number：21019329. E-mail：zdycf@pqcvlyfa.biz.cn

22。姓名：生王绅

住址（酒店）：广西壮族自治区钦州市钦南区金禹路 316 号坚嘉酒店（邮政编码：487235）。联系电话：64211967。电子邮箱：cldwe@yahqwoju.biz.cn

Zhù zhǐ: Shēng Wàng Shēn Guǎngxī Zhuàngzú Zìzhìqū Qīnzhōu Shì Qīn Nán Qū Jīn Yǔ Lù 316 Hào Jiān Jiā Jiǔ Diàn（Yóuzhèng Biānmǎ：487235). Liánxì Diànhuà：64211967. Diànzǐ Yóuxiāng：cldwe@yahqwoju.biz.cn

Wang Shen Sheng, Jian Jia Hotel, 316 Jin Yu Road, Chennan District, Qinzhou, Guangxi Autonomous Region. Postal Code: 487235. Phone Number：64211967. E-mail：cldwe@yahqwoju.biz.cn

23。姓名：家守乐

住址（湖泊）：广西壮族自治区梧州市苍梧县坚土路 473 号食跃湖（邮政编码：681250）。联系电话：55175996。电子邮箱：curzl@ocglwhsi.lakes.cn

Zhù zhǐ: Jiā Shǒu Lè Guǎngxī Zhuàngzú Zìzhìqū Wúzhōu Shì Cāng Wú Xiàn Jiān Tǔ Lù 473 Hào Yì Yuè Hú（Yóuzhèng Biānmǎ：681250). Liánxì Diànhuà：55175996. Diànzǐ Yóuxiāng：curzl@ocglwhsi.lakes.cn

Shou Le Jia, Yi Yue Lake, 473 Jian Tu Road, Cangwu County, Wuzhou, Guangxi Autonomous Region. Postal Code: 681250. Phone Number：55175996. E-mail：curzl@ocglwhsi.lakes.cn

24。姓名：程陶大

住址（酒店）：广西壮族自治区南宁市武鸣区领隆路 990 号光彬酒店（邮政编码：794434）。联系电话：21564899。电子邮箱：jopgn@owgfczrm.biz.cn

Zhù zhǐ: Chéng Táo Dà Guǎngxī Zhuàngzú Zìzhìqū Nánníng Shì Wǔ Míng Qū Lǐng Lóng Lù 990 Hào Guāng Bīn Jiǔ Diàn (Yóuzhèng Biānmǎ：794434). Liánxì Diànhuà：21564899. Diànzǐ Yóuxiāng：jopgn@owgfczrm.biz.cn

Tao Da Cheng, Guang Bin Hotel, 990 Ling Long Road, Wuming District, NanNing, Guangxi Autonomous Region. Postal Code: 794434. Phone Number：21564899. E-mail：jopgn@owgfczrm.biz.cn

25。姓名: 经焯柱

住址（家庭）：广西壮族自治区贵港市港北区可克路 868 号石隆公寓 38 层 803 室（邮政编码：557819）。联系电话：52375028。电子邮箱：fkaiu@vzuncyhw.cn

Zhù zhǐ: Jīng Zhuō Zhù Guǎngxī Zhuàngzú Zìzhìqū Guìgǎng Shì Gǎngběi Qū Kě Kè Lù 868 Hào Shí Lóng Gōng Yù 38 Céng 803 Shì (Yóuzhèng Biānmǎ：557819). Liánxì Diànhuà：52375028. Diànzǐ Yóuxiāng：fkaiu@vzuncyhw.cn

Zhuo Zhu Jing, Room# 803, Floor# 38, Shi Long Apartment, 868 Ke Ke Road, Gangbei District, Guigang, Guangxi Autonomous Region. Postal Code: 557819. Phone Number：52375028. E-mail：fkaiu@vzuncyhw.cn

26。姓名: 束帆坡

住址（医院）：广西壮族自治区防城港市港口区亚熔路 942 号白彬医院（邮政编码：686848）。联系电话：31648667。电子邮箱：ebqjk@ditluejx.health.cn

Zhù zhǐ: Shù Fān Pō Guǎngxī Zhuàngzú Zìzhìqū Fángchénggǎng Shì Gǎngkǒu Qū Yà Róng Lù 942 Hào Bái Bīn Yī Yuàn (Yóuzhèng Biānmǎ：686848). Liánxì Diànhuà：31648667. Diànzǐ Yóuxiāng：ebqjk@ditluejx.health.cn

Fan Po Shu, Bai Bin Hospital, 942 Ya Rong Road, Port Area, Fangchenggang, Guangxi Autonomous Region. Postal Code: 686848. Phone Number：31648667. E-mail：ebqjk@ditluejx.health.cn

27。姓名: 关晗仓

住址（酒店）：广西壮族自治区防城港市港口区其守路 261 号寰洵酒店（邮政编码：805797）。联系电话：52132395。电子邮箱：
jlmbw@imzklrxd.biz.cn

Zhù zhǐ: Guān Hán Cāng Guǎngxī Zhuàngzú Zìzhìqū Fángchénggǎng Shì Gǎngkǒu Qū Qí Shǒu Lù 261 Hào Huán Xún Jiǔ Diàn （Yóuzhèng Biānmǎ：805797). Liánxì Diànhuà：52132395. Diànzǐ Yóuxiāng：jlmbw@imzklrxd.biz.cn

Han Cang Guan, Huan Xun Hotel, 261 Qi Shou Road, Port Area, Fangchenggang, Guangxi Autonomous Region. Postal Code: 805797. Phone Number：52132395. E-mail：jlmbw@imzklrxd.biz.cn

28。姓名: 卢珂胜

住址（医院）：广西壮族自治区百色市隆林各族自治县德际路 774 号居智医院（邮政编码：388564）。联系电话：38751174。电子邮箱：
bucmz@uhyxcjlz.health.cn

Zhù zhǐ: Lú Kē Shēng Guǎngxī Zhuàngzú Zìzhìqū Bǎisè Shì Lóng Lín Gè Zú Zìzhìxiàn Dé Jì Lù 774 Hào Jū Zhì Yī Yuàn （Yóuzhèng Biānmǎ：388564). Liánxì Diànhuà：38751174. Diànzǐ Yóuxiāng：bucmz@uhyxcjlz.health.cn

Ke Sheng Lu, Ju Zhi Hospital, 774 De Ji Road, Longlin Autonomous County Of Various Nationalities, Baise, Guangxi Autonomous Region. Postal Code: 388564. Phone Number：38751174. E-mail：bucmz@uhyxcjlz.health.cn

29。姓名: 宇文尚顺

住址（医院）：广西壮族自治区百色市靖西市炯自路 578 号其风医院（邮政编码：678475）。联系电话：81332434。电子邮箱：
jcpsz@gzydpwjx.health.cn

Zhù zhǐ: Yǔwén Shàng Shùn Guǎngxī Zhuàngzú Zìzhìqū Bǎisè Shì Jìng Xī Shì Jiǒng Zì Lù 578 Hào Qí Fēng Yī Yuàn （Yóuzhèng Biānmǎ：678475). Liánxì Diànhuà：81332434. Diànzǐ Yóuxiāng：jcpsz@gzydpwjx.health.cn

Shang Shun Yuwen, Qi Feng Hospital, 578 Jiong Zi Road, Jingxi, Baise, Guangxi Autonomous Region. Postal Code: 678475. Phone Number：81332434. E-mail：jcpsz@gzydpwjx.health.cn

30。姓名:滑稼威

住址（湖泊）：广西壮族自治区梧州市万秀区钢翰路 351 号豹食湖（邮政编码：913462）。联系电话：90892137。电子邮箱：iokre@tonzhjmk.lakes.cn

Zhù zhǐ: Huá Jià Wēi Guǎngxī Zhuàngzú Zìzhìqū Wúzhōu Shì Wàn Xiù Qū Gāng Hàn Lù 351 Hào Bào Sì Hú （Yóuzhèng Biānmǎ：913462). Liánxì Diànhuà：90892137. Diànzǐ Yóuxiāng：iokre@tonzhjmk.lakes.cn

Jia Wei Hua, Bao Si Lake, 351 Gang Han Road, Wanxiu District, Wuzhou, Guangxi Autonomous Region. Postal Code: 913462. Phone Number：90892137. E-mail：iokre@tonzhjmk.lakes.cn

CHAPTER 2: NAME, SURNAME & ADDRESSES (31-60)

31。姓名: 顾郁迅

住址（家庭）：广西壮族自治区来宾市忻城县陆宝路 755 号南际公寓 50 层 900 室（邮政编码：815379）。联系电话：91378428。电子邮箱：izjpm@mcyovwlu.cn

Zhù zhǐ: Gù Yù Xùn Guǎngxī Zhuàngzú Zìzhìqū Láibīn Shì Xīn Chéng Xiàn Liù Bǎo Lù 755 Hào Nán Jì Gōng Yù 50 Céng 900 Shì (Yóuzhèng Biānmǎ：815379). Liánxì Diànhuà：91378428. Diànzǐ Yóuxiāng：izjpm@mcyovwlu.cn

Yu Xun Gu, Room# 900, Floor# 50, Nan Ji Apartment, 755 Liu Bao Road, Xincheng County, Laibin, Guangxi Autonomous Region. Postal Code: 815379. Phone Number：91378428. E-mail：izjpm@mcyovwlu.cn

32。姓名: 亓官居淹

住址（家庭）：广西壮族自治区百色市平果市辉山路 281 号九毅公寓 46 层 219 室（邮政编码：481773）。联系电话：35533202。电子邮箱：wubqo@cvydiesh.cn

Zhù zhǐ: Qíguān Jū Yān Guǎngxī Zhuàngzú Zìzhìqū Bǎisè Shì Píng Guǒ Shì Huī Shān Lù 281 Hào Jiǔ Yì Gōng Yù 46 Céng 219 Shì (Yóuzhèng Biānmǎ：481773). Liánxì Diànhuà：35533202. Diànzǐ Yóuxiāng：wubqo@cvydiesh.cn

Ju Yan Qiguan, Room# 219, Floor# 46, Jiu Yi Apartment, 281 Hui Shan Road, Pingguo City, Baise, Guangxi Autonomous Region. Postal Code: 481773. Phone Number：35533202. E-mail：wubqo@cvydiesh.cn

33。姓名: 微敬大

住址（博物院）：广西壮族自治区来宾市合山市国盛路 488 号来宾博物馆（邮政编码：336009）。联系电话：15723108。电子邮箱：dobwj@txanmjvc.museums.cn

Zhù zhǐ: Wēi Jìng Dài Guǎngxī Zhuàngzú Zìzhìqū Láibīn Shì Hé Shān Shì Guó Shèng Lù 488 Hào Láibīn Bó Wù Guǎn (Yóuzhèng Biānmǎ：336009). Liánxì Diànhuà：15723108. Diànzǐ Yóuxiāng：dobwj@txanmjvc.museums.cn

Jing Dai Wei, Laibin Museum, 488 Guo Sheng Road, Heshan City, Laibin, Guangxi Autonomous Region. Postal Code: 336009. Phone Number：15723108. E-mail：dobwj@txanmjvc.museums.cn

34。姓名: 太叔水珂

住址（火车站）：广西壮族自治区玉林市玉州区化计路 541 号玉林站（邮政编码：356657）。联系电话：22983566。电子邮箱：jemdt@qkpeyiof.chr.cn

Zhù zhǐ: Tàishū Shuǐ Kē Guǎngxī Zhuàngzú Zìzhìqū Yùlín Shì Yù Zhōu Qū Huā Jì Lù 541 Hào Yùlín Zhàn (Yóuzhèng Biānmǎ：356657). Liánxì Diànhuà：22983566. Diànzǐ Yóuxiāng：jemdt@qkpeyiof.chr.cn

Shui Ke Taishu, Yulin Railway Station, 541 Hua Ji Road, Yuzhou District, Yulin, Guangxi Autonomous Region. Postal Code: 356657. Phone Number：22983566. E-mail：jemdt@qkpeyiof.chr.cn

35。姓名: 钭兆葆

住址（火车站）：广西壮族自治区贵港市港北区食葛路 587 号贵港站（邮政编码：717839）。联系电话：23998351。电子邮箱：zkqia@vuchrpmn.chr.cn

Zhù zhǐ: Tǒu Zhào Bǎo Guǎngxī Zhuàngzú Zìzhìqū Guìgǎng Shì Gǎngběi Qū Yì Gé Lù 587 Hào Gugǎng Zhàn (Yóuzhèng Biānmǎ：717839). Liánxì Diànhuà：23998351. Diànzǐ Yóuxiāng：zkqia@vuchrpmn.chr.cn

Zhao Bao Tou, Guigang Railway Station, 587 Yi Ge Road, Gangbei District, Guigang, Guangxi Autonomous Region. Postal Code: 717839. Phone Number：23998351. E-mail：zkqia@vuchrpmn.chr.cn

36。姓名: 东郭食宽

住址（医院）：广西壮族自治区桂林市永福县洶九路 571 号晖土医院（邮政编码：324961）。联系电话：26548119。电子邮箱：nxvgu@uaotxvys.health.cn

Zhù zhǐ: Dōngguō Sì Kuān Guǎngxī Zhuàngzú Zìzhìqū Guìlín Shì Yǒngfú Xiàn Xún Jiǔ Lù 571 Hào Huī Tǔ Yī Yuàn（Yóuzhèng Biānmǎ：324961). Liánxì Diànhuà：26548119. Diànzǐ Yóuxiāng：nxvgu@uaotxvys.health.cn

Si Kuan Dongguo, Hui Tu Hospital, 571 Xun Jiu Road, Yongfu County, Guilin, Guangxi Autonomous Region. Postal Code: 324961. Phone Number：26548119. E-mail：nxvgu@uaotxvys.health.cn

37。姓名: 罗泽独

住址（机场）：广西壮族自治区玉林市玉州区鸣桥路 904 号玉林中启国际机场（邮政编码：950750）。联系电话：65592519。电子邮箱：waeij@knpxolej.airports.cn

Zhù zhǐ: Luó Zé Dú Guǎngxī Zhuàngzú Zìzhìqū Yùlín Shì Yù Zhōu Qū Míng Qiáo Lù 904 Hào Yùlín Zhōng Qǐ Guó Jì Jī Chǎng（Yóuzhèng Biānmǎ：950750). Liánxì Diànhuà：65592519. Diànzǐ Yóuxiāng：waeij@knpxolej.airports.cn

Ze Du Luo, Yulin Zhong Qi International Airport, 904 Ming Qiao Road, Yuzhou District, Yulin, Guangxi Autonomous Region. Postal Code: 950750. Phone Number：65592519. E-mail：waeij@knpxolej.airports.cn

38。姓名: 言自钢

住址（寺庙）：广西壮族自治区来宾市忻城县翰轶路 658 号翼祥寺（邮政编码：699723）。联系电话：29982021。电子邮箱：rhwio@kyhfucar.god.cn

Zhù zhǐ: Yán Zì Gāng Guǎngxī Zhuàngzú Zìzhìqū Láibīn Shì Xīn Chéng Xiàn Hàn Yì Lù 658 Hào Yì Xiáng Sì（Yóuzhèng Biānmǎ：699723). Liánxì Diànhuà：29982021. Diànzǐ Yóuxiāng：rhwio@kyhfucar.god.cn

Zi Gang Yan, Yi Xiang Temple, 658 Han Yi Road, Xincheng County, Laibin, Guangxi Autonomous Region. Postal Code: 699723. Phone Number：29982021. E-mail：rhwio@kyhfucar.god.cn

39。姓名：汝中九

住址（酒店）：广西壮族自治区来宾市合山市帆福路 408 号豪发酒店（邮政编码：961381）。联系电话：38942850。电子邮箱：qblxw@xunmrvcq.biz.cn

Zhù zhǐ: Rǔ Zhōng Jiǔ Guǎngxī Zhuàngzú Zìzhìqū Láibīn Shì Hé Shān Shì Fān Fú Lù 408 Hào Háo Fā Jiǔ Diàn（Yóuzhèng Biānmǎ：961381). Liánxì Diànhuà：38942850. Diànzǐ Yóuxiāng：qblxw@xunmrvcq.biz.cn

Zhong Jiu Ru, Hao Fa Hotel, 408 Fan Fu Road, Heshan City, Laibin, Guangxi Autonomous Region. Postal Code: 961381. Phone Number：38942850. E-mail：qblxw@xunmrvcq.biz.cn

40。姓名：邱继豪

住址（火车站）：广西壮族自治区崇左市龙州县尚食路 276 号崇左站（邮政编码：504636）。联系电话：12027943。电子邮箱：mrifa@pegkzwmd.chr.cn

Zhù zhǐ: Qiū Jì Háo Guǎngxī Zhuàngzú Zìzhìqū Chóng Zuǒ Shì Lóng Zhōu Xiàn Shàng Shí Lù 276 Hào Cóng Zuǒ Zhàn（Yóuzhèng Biānmǎ：504636). Liánxì Diànhuà：12027943. Diànzǐ Yóuxiāng：mrifa@pegkzwmd.chr.cn

Ji Hao Qiu, Chongzuo Railway Station, 276 Shang Shi Road, Longzhou County, Chongzuo, Guangxi Autonomous Region. Postal Code: 504636. Phone Number：12027943. E-mail：mrifa@pegkzwmd.chr.cn

41。姓名：简强土

住址（博物院）：广西壮族自治区柳州市柳江区焯歧路 872 号柳州博物馆（邮政编码：729287）。联系电话：22538287。电子邮箱：gizbk@fbkalomw.museums.cn

Zhù zhǐ: Jiǎn Qiǎng Tǔ Guǎngxī Zhuàngzú Zìzhìqū Liǔzhōu Shì Liǔjiāng Qū Chāo Qí Lù 872 Hào Liǔzōu Bó Wù Guǎn（Yóuzhèng Biānmǎ：729287). Liánxì Diànhuà：22538287. Diànzǐ Yóuxiāng：gizbk@fbkalomw.museums.cn

Qiang Tu Jian, Liuzhou Museum, 872 Chao Qi Road, Liujiang District, Liuzhou, Guangxi Autonomous Region. Postal Code: 729287. Phone Number：22538287. E-mail：gizbk@fbkalomw.museums.cn

42。姓名: 习科启

住址（博物院）：广西壮族自治区河池市金城江区院腾路 141 号河池博物馆（邮政编码：175804）。联系电话：70835247。电子邮箱：djtnk@vjxkzdfo.museums.cn

Zhù zhǐ: Xí Kē Qǐ Guǎngxī Zhuàngzú Zìzhìqū Héchí Shì Jīnchéng Jiāng Qū Yuàn Téng Lù 141 Hào Hécí Bó Wù Guǎn（Yóuzhèng Biānmǎ：175804). Liánxì Diànhuà：70835247. Diànzǐ Yóuxiāng：djtnk@vjxkzdfo.museums.cn

Ke Qi Xi, Hechi Museum, 141 Yuan Teng Road, Jinchengjiang District, Hechi, Guangxi Autonomous Region. Postal Code: 175804. Phone Number：70835247. E-mail：djtnk@vjxkzdfo.museums.cn

43。姓名: 司寇陆腾

住址（广场）：广西壮族自治区柳州市三江侗族自治县源懂路 123 号计化广场（邮政编码：949686）。联系电话：42401589。电子邮箱：kqdgx@qsbkgcru.squares.cn

Zhù zhǐ: Sīkòu Liù Téng Guǎngxī Zhuàngzú Zìzhìqū Liǔzhōu Shì Sānjiāng Dòngzú Zìzhìxiàn Yuán Dǒng Lù 123 Hào Jì Huā Guǎng Chǎng（Yóuzhèng Biānmǎ：949686). Liánxì Diànhuà：42401589. Diànzǐ Yóuxiāng：kqdgx@qsbkgcru.squares.cn

Liu Teng Sikou, Ji Hua Square, 123 Yuan Dong Road, Sanjiang Dong Autonomous County, Liuzhou, Guangxi Autonomous Region. Postal Code: 949686. Phone Number：42401589. E-mail：kqdgx@qsbkgcru.squares.cn

44。姓名: 唐彬际

住址（寺庙）：广西壮族自治区柳州市鱼峰区珏钦路 982 号懂庆寺（邮政编码：584909）。联系电话：86130838。电子邮箱：jdvwl@bmarjnyd.god.cn

Zhù zhǐ: Táng Bīn Jì Guǎngxī Zhuàngzú Zìzhìqū Liǔzhōu Shì Yú Fēng Qū Jué Qīn Lù 982 Hào Dǒng Qìng Sì (Yóuzhèng Biānmǎ：584909). Liánxì Diànhuà：86130838. Diànzǐ Yóuxiāng：jdvwl@bmarjnyd.god.cn

Bin Ji Tang, Dong Qing Temple, 982 Jue Qin Road, Yufeng District, Liuzhou, Guangxi Autonomous Region. Postal Code: 584909. Phone Number：86130838. E-mail：jdvwl@bmarjnyd.god.cn

45。姓名: 昝星食

住址（广场）：广西壮族自治区防城港市上思县葆舟路 817 号龙员广场（邮政编码：881833）。联系电话：54408543。电子邮箱：rxmfy@gmsbdwxr.squares.cn

Zhù zhǐ: Zǎn Xīng Sì Guǎngxī Zhuàngzú Zìzhìqū Fángchénggǎng Shì Shàng Sī Xiàn Bǎo Zhōu Lù 817 Hào Lóng Yún Guǎng Chǎng (Yóuzhèng Biānmǎ：881833). Liánxì Diànhuà：54408543. Diànzǐ Yóuxiāng：rxmfy@gmsbdwxr.squares.cn

Xing Si Zan, Long Yun Square, 817 Bao Zhou Road, Shangsi County, Fangchenggang, Guangxi Autonomous Region. Postal Code: 881833. Phone Number：54408543. E-mail：rxmfy@gmsbdwxr.squares.cn

46。姓名: 姬熔铭

住址（火车站）：广西壮族自治区北海市银海区可山路 763 号北海站（邮政编码：365124）。联系电话：71246078。电子邮箱：emnxd@pfduzhgs.chr.cn

Zhù zhǐ: Jī Róng Míng Guǎngxī Zhuàngzú Zìzhìqū Běihǎi Shì Yín Hǎi Qū Kě Shān Lù 763 Hào Běiǎi Zhàn (Yóuzhèng Biānmǎ：365124). Liánxì Diànhuà：71246078. Diànzǐ Yóuxiāng：emnxd@pfduzhgs.chr.cn

Rong Ming Ji, Beihai Railway Station, 763 Ke Shan Road, Yinhai District, Beihai, Guangxi Autonomous Region. Postal Code: 365124. Phone Number：71246078. E-mail：emnxd@pfduzhgs.chr.cn

47。姓名: 颜山惟

住址（医院）：广西壮族自治区北海市合浦县食禹路 507 号谢院医院（邮政编码：152690）。联系电话：12572508。电子邮箱：jzlvg@nvbeqktw.health.cn

Zhù zhǐ: Yán Shān Wéi Guǎngxī Zhuàngzú Zìzhìqū Běihǎi Shì Hépǔ Xiàn Shí Yǔ Lù 507 Hào Xiè Yuàn Yī Yuàn (Yóuzhèng Biānmǎ：152690). Liánxì Diànhuà：12572508. Diànzǐ Yóuxiāng：jzlvg@nvbeqktw.health.cn

Shan Wei Yan, Xie Yuan Hospital, 507 Shi Yu Road, Hepu County, Beihai, Guangxi Autonomous Region. Postal Code: 152690. Phone Number：12572508. E-mail：jzlvg@nvbeqktw.health.cn

48。姓名: 诸易化

住址（大学）：广西壮族自治区防城港市东兴市乙近大学智化路 966 号（邮政编码：259062）。联系电话：91616187。电子邮箱：lcfjr@fntzmqbx.edu.cn

Zhù zhǐ: Zhū Yì Huà Guǎngxī Zhuàngzú Zìzhìqū Fángchénggǎng Shì Dōng Xīng Shì Yǐ Jìn DàxuéZhì Huā Lù 966 Hào (Yóuzhèng Biānmǎ：259062). Liánxì Diànhuà：91616187. Diànzǐ Yóuxiāng：lcfjr@fntzmqbx.edu.cn

Yi Hua Zhu, Yi Jin University, 966 Zhi Hua Road, Dongxing City, Fangchenggang, Guangxi Autonomous Region. Postal Code: 259062. Phone Number：91616187. E-mail：lcfjr@fntzmqbx.edu.cn

49。姓名: 师星领

住址（大学）：广西壮族自治区来宾市武宣县院独大学独智路 104 号（邮政编码：648922）。联系电话：57876936。电子邮箱：bxmpk@sfzntkpj.edu.cn

Zhù zhǐ: Shī Xīng Lǐng Guǎngxī Zhuàngzú Zìzhìqū Láibīn Shì Wǔxuān Xiàn Yuàn Dú DàxuéDú Zhì Lù 104 Hào（Yóuzhèng Biānmǎ：648922）. Liánxì Diànhuà：57876936. Diànzǐ Yóuxiāng：bxmpk@sfzntkpj.edu.cn

Xing Ling Shi, Yuan Du University, 104 Du Zhi Road, Wuxuan County, Laibin, Guangxi Autonomous Region. Postal Code: 648922. Phone Number：57876936. E-mail：bxmpk@sfzntkpj.edu.cn

50。姓名: 益土独

住址（大学）：广西壮族自治区玉林市玉州区中沛大学人冠路 792 号（邮政编码：860553）。联系电话：72011812。电子邮箱：glmrc@mdhqjprz.edu.cn

Zhù zhǐ: Yì Tǔ Dú Guǎngxī Zhuàngzú Zìzhìqū Yùlín Shì Yù Zhōu Qū Zhōng Pèi DàxuéRén Guàn Lù 792 Hào（Yóuzhèng Biānmǎ：860553）. Liánxì Diànhuà：72011812. Diànzǐ Yóuxiāng：glmrc@mdhqjprz.edu.cn

Tu Du Yi, Zhong Pei University, 792 Ren Guan Road, Yuzhou District, Yulin, Guangxi Autonomous Region. Postal Code: 860553. Phone Number：72011812. E-mail：glmrc@mdhqjprz.edu.cn

51。姓名: 郏亮涛

住址（博物院）：广西壮族自治区南宁市武鸣区仓智路 616 号南宁博物馆（邮政编码：837427）。联系电话：73721791。电子邮箱：vnlrz@gbuwsdvt.museums.cn

Zhù zhǐ: Jiá Liàng Tāo Guǎngxī Zhuàngzú Zìzhìqū Nánníng Shì Wǔ Míng Qū Cāng Zhì Lù 616 Hào Nánníng Bó Wù Guǎn（Yóuzhèng Biānmǎ：837427）. Liánxì Diànhuà：73721791. Diànzǐ Yóuxiāng：vnlrz@gbuwsdvt.museums.cn

Liang Tao Jia, NanNing Museum, 616 Cang Zhi Road, Wuming District, NanNing, Guangxi Autonomous Region. Postal Code: 837427. Phone Number：73721791. E-mail：vnlrz@gbuwsdvt.museums.cn

52。姓名: 蔡庆不

住址（医院）：广西壮族自治区贺州市富川瑶族自治县员中路 740 号兆楚医院（邮政编码：538882）。联系电话：40565895。电子邮箱：vcgyh@fmwxyhua.health.cn

Zhù zhǐ: Cài Qìng Bù Guǎngxī Zhuàngzú Zìzhìqū Hèzhōu Shì Fùchuān Yáozú Zìzhìxiàn Yún Zhòng Lù 740 Hào Zhào Chǔ Yī Yuàn（Yóuzhèng Biānmǎ：538882). Liánxì Diànhuà：40565895. Diànzǐ Yóuxiāng：vcgyh@fmwxyhua.health.cn

Qing Bu Cai, Zhao Chu Hospital, 740 Yun Zhong Road, Fuchuan Yao Autonomous County, Hezhou, Guangxi Autonomous Region. Postal Code: 538882. Phone Number：40565895. E-mail：vcgyh@fmwxyhua.health.cn

53。姓名: 武辉成

住址（公司）：广西壮族自治区贺州市昭平县己风路 794 号世冕有限公司（邮政编码：170269）。联系电话：51350005。电子邮箱：fgoup@dthnyjie.biz.cn

Zhù zhǐ: Wǔ Huī Chéng Guǎngxī Zhuàngzú Zìzhìqū Hèzhōu Shì Zhāopíng Xiàn Jǐ Fēng Lù 794 Hào Shì Miǎn Yǒuxiàn Gōngsī（Yóuzhèng Biānmǎ：170269). Liánxì Diànhuà：51350005. Diànzǐ Yóuxiāng：fgoup@dthnyjie.biz.cn

Hui Cheng Wu, Shi Mian Corporation, 794 Ji Feng Road, Zhaoping County, Hezhou, Guangxi Autonomous Region. Postal Code: 170269. Phone Number：51350005. E-mail：fgoup@dthnyjie.biz.cn

54。姓名: 余柱咚

住址（火车站）：广西壮族自治区柳州市城中区计亚路 233 号柳州站（邮政编码：986568）。联系电话：37139352。电子邮箱：pqvzr@oajfzrun.chr.cn

Zhù zhǐ: Yú Zhù Dōng Guǎngxī Zhuàngzú Zìzhìqū Liǔzhōu Shì Chéngzhōng Qū Jì Yà Lù 233 Hào Liǔzōu Zhàn (Yóuzhèng Biānmǎ：986568). Liánxì Diànhuà：37139352. Diànzǐ Yóuxiāng：pqvzr@oajfzrun.chr.cn

Zhu Dong Yu, Liuzhou Railway Station, 233 Ji Ya Road, Chengzhong District, Liuzhou, Guangxi Autonomous Region. Postal Code: 986568. Phone Number：37139352. E-mail：pqvzr@oajfzrun.chr.cn

55。姓名: 瞿化龙

住址（博物院）：广西壮族自治区来宾市忻城县辙德路 669 号来宾博物馆（邮政编码：956431）。联系电话：73456313。电子邮箱：yvtos@ikjqfmby.museums.cn

Zhù zhǐ: Qú Huà Lóng Guǎngxī Zhuàngzú Zìzhìqū Láibīn Shì Xīn Chéng Xiàn Zhé Dé Lù 669 Hào Láibīn Bó Wù Guǎn (Yóuzhèng Biānmǎ：956431). Liánxì Diànhuà：73456313. Diànzǐ Yóuxiāng：yvtos@ikjqfmby.museums.cn

Hua Long Qu, Laibin Museum, 669 Zhe De Road, Xincheng County, Laibin, Guangxi Autonomous Region. Postal Code: 956431. Phone Number：73456313. E-mail：yvtos@ikjqfmby.museums.cn

56。姓名: 南门土成

住址（大学）：广西壮族自治区柳州市鱼峰区奎尚大学铭食路 767 号（邮政编码：581290）。联系电话：36727963。电子邮箱：xmikv@ohbrmanv.edu.cn

Zhù zhǐ: Nánmén Tǔ Chéng Guǎngxī Zhuàngzú Zìzhìqū Liǔzhōu Shì Yú Fēng Qū Kuí Shàng DàxuéMíng Sì Lù 767 Hào (Yóuzhèng Biānmǎ：581290). Liánxì Diànhuà：36727963. Diànzǐ Yóuxiāng：xmikv@ohbrmanv.edu.cn

Tu Cheng Nanmen, Kui Shang University, 767 Ming Si Road, Yufeng District, Liuzhou, Guangxi Autonomous Region. Postal Code: 581290. Phone Number：36727963. E-mail：xmikv@ohbrmanv.edu.cn

57。姓名: 应可威

住址（火车站）：广西壮族自治区河池市凤山县威豹路 459 号河池站（邮政编码：540929）。联系电话：66674662。电子邮箱：xpzes@gcemkfwq.chr.cn

Zhù zhǐ: Yīng Kě Wēi Guǎngxī Zhuàngzú Zìzhìqū Héchí Shì Fèng Shān Xiàn Wēi Bào Lù 459 Hào Hécí Zhàn（Yóuzhèng Biānmǎ：540929). Liánxì Diànhuà：66674662. Diànzǐ Yóuxiāng：xpzes@gcemkfwq.chr.cn

Ke Wei Ying, Hechi Railway Station, 459 Wei Bao Road, Fengshan County, Hechi, Guangxi Autonomous Region. Postal Code: 540929. Phone Number：66674662. E-mail：xpzes@gcemkfwq.chr.cn

58。姓名: 於隆智

住址（大学）：广西壮族自治区崇左市天等县泽原大学金仓路 291 号（邮政编码：934772）。联系电话：14993606。电子邮箱：vhmux@jltinkrh.edu.cn

Zhù zhǐ: Yū Lóng Zhì Guǎngxī Zhuàngzú Zìzhìqū Chóng Zuǒ Shì Tiān Děng Xiàn Zé Yuán DàxuéJīn Cāng Lù 291 Hào（Yóuzhèng Biānmǎ：934772). Liánxì Diànhuà：14993606. Diànzǐ Yóuxiāng：vhmux@jltinkrh.edu.cn

Long Zhi Yu, Ze Yuan University, 291 Jin Cang Road, Tiandeng County, Chongzuo, Guangxi Autonomous Region. Postal Code: 934772. Phone Number：14993606. E-mail：vhmux@jltinkrh.edu.cn

59。姓名: 滑辙国

住址（公园）：广西壮族自治区防城港市港口区大翰路 617 号祥征公园（邮政编码：163882）。联系电话：67541970。电子邮箱：xzoft@ualmibnq.parks.cn

Zhù zhǐ: Huá Zhé Guó Guǎngxī Zhuàngzú Zìzhìqū Fángchénggǎng Shì Gǎngkǒu Qū Dà Hàn Lù 617 Hào Xiáng Zhēng Gōng Yuán（Yóuzhèng Biānmǎ：163882). Liánxì Diànhuà：67541970. Diànzǐ Yóuxiāng：xzoft@ualmibnq.parks.cn

Zhe Guo Hua, Xiang Zheng Park, 617 Da Han Road, Port Area, Fangchenggang, Guangxi Autonomous Region. Postal Code: 163882. Phone Number：67541970. E-mail：xzoft@ualmibnq.parks.cn

60。姓名: 雍腾庆

住址（博物院）：广西壮族自治区贵港市桂平市冠员路 830 号贵港博物馆（邮政编码：281188）。联系电话：28963749。电子邮箱：tidjs@lufjnxir.museums.cn

Zhù zhǐ: Yōng Téng Qìng Guǎngxī Zhuàngzú Zìzhìqū Guìgǎng Shì Guìpíngshì Guàn Yuán Lù 830 Hào Gugǎng Bó Wù Guǎn (Yóuzhèng Biānmǎ：281188). Liánxì Diànhuà：28963749. Diànzǐ Yóuxiāng：tidjs@lufjnxir.museums.cn

Teng Qing Yong, Guigang Museum, 830 Guan Yuan Road, Guiping, Guigang, Guangxi Autonomous Region. Postal Code: 281188. Phone Number：28963749. E-mail：tidjs@lufjnxir.museums.cn

61。姓名: 骆化来

住址（家庭）：广西壮族自治区柳州市柳北区先乐路 801 号绅愈公寓 23 层 855 室（邮政编码：340423）。联系电话：28753766。电子邮箱：junrq@gdhacvyb.cn

Zhù zhǐ: Luò Huà Lái Guǎngxī Zhuàngzú Zìzhìqū Liǔzhōu Shì Liǔběi Qū Xiān Lè Lù 801 Hào Shēn Yù Gōng Yù 23 Céng 855 Shì (Yóuzhèng Biānmǎ：340423). Liánxì Diànhuà：28753766. Diànzǐ Yóuxiāng：junrq@gdhacvyb.cn

Hua Lai Luo, Room# 855, Floor# 23, Shen Yu Apartment, 801 Xian Le Road, Liubei District, Liuzhou, Guangxi Autonomous Region. Postal Code: 340423. Phone Number：28753766. E-mail：junrq@gdhacvyb.cn

62。姓名: 张乐陶

住址（湖泊）：广西壮族自治区柳州市柳北区郁亭路 144 号光辉湖（邮政编码：339236）。联系电话：37032775。电子邮箱：svtdc@pfthokzw.lakes.cn

Zhù zhǐ: Zhāng Lè Táo Guǎngxī Zhuàngzú Zìzhìqū Liǔzhōu Shì Liǔběi Qū Yù Tíng Lù 144 Hào Guāng Huī Hú (Yóuzhèng Biānmǎ：339236). Liánxì Diànhuà：37032775. Diànzǐ Yóuxiāng：svtdc@pfthokzw.lakes.cn

Le Tao Zhang, Guang Hui Lake, 144 Yu Ting Road, Liubei District, Liuzhou, Guangxi Autonomous Region. Postal Code: 339236. Phone Number：37032775. E-mail：svtdc@pfthokzw.lakes.cn

63。姓名: 蓝毅民

住址（广场）：广西壮族自治区贵港市港北区秀愈路 823 号豹郁广场（邮政编码：558096）。联系电话：49220601。电子邮箱：jiphn@fpchzygi.squares.cn

Zhù zhǐ: Lán Yì Mín Guǎngxī Zhuàngzú Zìzhìqū Guìgǎng Shì Gǎngběi Qū Xiù Yù Lù 823 Hào Bào Yù Guǎng Chǎng（Yóuzhèng Biānmǎ：558096). Liánxì Diànhuà：49220601. Diànzǐ Yóuxiāng：jiphn@fpchzygi.squares.cn

Yi Min Lan, Bao Yu Square, 823 Xiu Yu Road, Gangbei District, Guigang, Guangxi Autonomous Region. Postal Code: 558096. Phone Number：49220601. E-mail：jiphn@fpchzygi.squares.cn

64。姓名：蔺强游

住址（酒店）：广西壮族自治区崇左市龙州县恩继路 726 号秀强酒店（邮政编码：866715）。联系电话：65323385。电子邮箱：padfg@unkldjsb.biz.cn

Zhù zhǐ: Lìn Qiáng Yóu Guǎngxī Zhuàngzú Zìzhìqū Chóng Zuǒ Shì Lóng Zhōu Xiàn Ēn Jì Lù 726 Hào Xiù Qiáng Jiǔ Diàn（Yóuzhèng Biānmǎ：866715). Liánxì Diànhuà：65323385. Diànzǐ Yóuxiāng：padfg@unkldjsb.biz.cn

Qiang You Lin, Xiu Qiang Hotel, 726 En Ji Road, Longzhou County, Chongzuo, Guangxi Autonomous Region. Postal Code: 866715. Phone Number：65323385. E-mail：padfg@unkldjsb.biz.cn

65。姓名：乜嘉葛

住址（博物院）：广西壮族自治区钦州市钦南区沛星路 476 号钦州博物馆（邮政编码：758572）。联系电话：75540951。电子邮箱：gshir@ovphlrue.museums.cn

Zhù zhǐ: Niè Jiā Gé Guǎngxī Zhuàngzú Zìzhìqū Qīnzhōu Shì Qīn Nán Qū Pèi Xīng Lù 476 Hào Qīnzōu Bó Wù Guǎn（Yóuzhèng Biānmǎ：758572). Liánxì Diànhuà：75540951. Diànzǐ Yóuxiāng：gshir@ovphlrue.museums.cn

Jia Ge Nie, Qinzhou Museum, 476 Pei Xing Road, Chennan District, Qinzhou, Guangxi Autonomous Region. Postal Code: 758572. Phone Number：75540951. E-mail：gshir@ovphlrue.museums.cn

66。姓名：臧自员

住址（博物院）：广西壮族自治区来宾市兴宾区葛强路 118 号来宾博物馆（邮政编码：586087）。联系电话：77255286。电子邮箱：jeufw@sykctfao.museums.cn

Zhù zhǐ: Zāng Zì Yún Guǎngxī Zhuàngzú Zìzhìqū Láibīn Shì Xìng Bīn Qū Gé Qiáng Lù 118 Hào Láibīn Bó Wù Guǎn (Yóuzhèng Biānmǎ：586087). Liánxì Diànhuà：77255286. Diànzǐ Yóuxiāng：jeufw@sykctfao.museums.cn

Zi Yun Zang, Laibin Museum, 118 Ge Qiang Road, Xingbin District, Laibin, Guangxi Autonomous Region. Postal Code: 586087. Phone Number：77255286. E-mail：jeufw@sykctfao.museums.cn

67。姓名: 端木化迅

住址（家庭）：广西壮族自治区河池市天峨县译懂路 476 号葆桥公寓 4 层 287 室（邮政编码：772383）。联系电话：80145616。电子邮箱：dqcxk@jvuydnts.cn

Zhù zhǐ: Duānmù Huā Xùn Guǎngxī Zhuàngzú Zìzhìqū Héchí Shì Tiān É Xiàn Yì Dǒng Lù 476 Hào Bǎo Qiáo Gōng Yù 4 Céng 287 Shì (Yóuzhèng Biānmǎ：772383). Liánxì Diànhuà：80145616. Diànzǐ Yóuxiāng：dqcxk@jvuydnts.cn

Hua Xun Duanmu, Room# 287, Floor# 4, Bao Qiao Apartment, 476 Yi Dong Road, Tiane County, Hechi, Guangxi Autonomous Region. Postal Code: 772383. Phone Number：80145616. E-mail：dqcxk@jvuydnts.cn

68。姓名: 汝焯成

住址（酒店）：广西壮族自治区百色市乐业县舟惟路 687 号斌俊酒店（邮政编码：997560）。联系电话：83351836。电子邮箱：uzejn@knthzgsv.biz.cn

Zhù zhǐ: Rǔ Zhuō Chéng Guǎngxī Zhuàngzú Zìzhìqū Bǎisè Shì Lè Yè Xiàn Zhōu Wéi Lù 687 Hào Bīn Jùn Jiǔ Diàn (Yóuzhèng Biānmǎ：997560). Liánxì Diànhuà：83351836. Diànzǐ Yóuxiāng：uzejn@knthzgsv.biz.cn

Zhuo Cheng Ru, Bin Jun Hotel, 687 Zhou Wei Road, Leye County, Baise, Guangxi Autonomous Region. Postal Code: 997560. Phone Number：83351836. E-mail：uzejn@knthzgsv.biz.cn

69。姓名: 傅游乐

住址（大学）：广西壮族自治区百色市平果市龙隆大学兆民路 514 号（邮政编码：314972）。联系电话：92804643。电子邮箱：vkjuq@qtbsfkzj.edu.cn

Zhù zhǐ: Fù Yóu Lè Guǎngxī Zhuàngzú Zìzhìqū Bǎisè Shì Píng Guǒ Shì Lóng Lóng DàxuéZhào Mín Lù 514 Hào（Yóuzhèng Biānmǎ：314972). Liánxì Diànhuà：92804643. Diànzǐ Yóuxiāng：vkjuq@qtbsfkzj.edu.cn

You Le Fu, Long Long University, 514 Zhao Min Road, Pingguo City, Baise, Guangxi Autonomous Region. Postal Code: 314972. Phone Number：92804643. E-mail：vkjuq@qtbsfkzj.edu.cn

70。姓名: 宣盛臻

住址（公园）：广西壮族自治区桂林市临桂区食豪路 545 号彬威公园（邮政编码：427300）。联系电话：89262370。电子邮箱：suwti@vlgxswtz.parks.cn

Zhù zhǐ: Xuān Shèng Zhēn Guǎngxī Zhuàngzú Zìzhìqū Guìlín Shì Lín Guì Qū Shí Háo Lù 545 Hào Bīn Wēi Gōng Yuán（Yóuzhèng Biānmǎ：427300). Liánxì Diànhuà：89262370. Diànzǐ Yóuxiāng：suwti@vlgxswtz.parks.cn

Sheng Zhen Xuan, Bin Wei Park, 545 Shi Hao Road, Lingui District, Guilin, Guangxi Autonomous Region. Postal Code: 427300. Phone Number：89262370. E-mail：suwti@vlgxswtz.parks.cn

71。姓名: 轩辕原冠

住址（机场）：广西壮族自治区梧州市岑溪市懂锤路 646 号梧州甫员国际机场（邮政编码：718896）。联系电话：79953159。电子邮箱：vculh@hkqywruv.airports.cn

Zhù zhǐ: Xuānyuán Yuán Guàn Guǎngxī Zhuàngzú Zìzhìqū Wúzhōu Shì Cénxī Shì Dǒng Chuí Lù 646 Hào Wúzōu Fǔ Yuán Guó Jì Jī Chǎng (Yóuzhèng Biānmǎ：718896). Liánxì Diànhuà：79953159. Diànzǐ Yóuxiāng：vculh@hkqywruv.airports.cn

Yuan Guan Xuanyuan, Wuzhou Fu Yuan International Airport, 646 Dong Chui Road, Cenxi City, Wuzhou, Guangxi Autonomous Region. Postal Code: 718896. Phone Number：79953159. E-mail：vculh@hkqywruv.airports.cn

72。姓名: 琴鹤白

住址（湖泊）：广西壮族自治区防城港市上思县珏易路 165 号禹游湖（邮政编码：617958）。联系电话：88955126。电子邮箱：hflrc@bscrkmtv.lakes.cn

Zhù zhǐ: Qín Hè Bái Guǎngxī Zhuàngzú Zìzhìqū Fángchénggǎng Shì Shàng Sī Xiàn Jué Yì Lù 165 Hào Yǔ Yóu Hú (Yóuzhèng Biānmǎ：617958). Liánxì Diànhuà：88955126. Diànzǐ Yóuxiāng：hflrc@bscrkmtv.lakes.cn

He Bai Qin, Yu You Lake, 165 Jue Yi Road, Shangsi County, Fangchenggang, Guangxi Autonomous Region. Postal Code: 617958. Phone Number：88955126. E-mail：hflrc@bscrkmtv.lakes.cn

73。姓名: 赵胜圣

住址（广场）：广西壮族自治区河池市巴马瑶族自治县智晗路 364 号浩盛广场（邮政编码：828573）。联系电话：42334464。电子邮箱：zupct@opbedhvn.squares.cn

Zhù zhǐ: Zhào Shēng Shèng Guǎngxī Zhuàngzú Zìzhìqū Héchí Shì Bā Mǎ Yáozú Zìzhìxiàn Zhì Hán Lù 364 Hào Hào Chéng Guǎng Chǎng (Yóuzhèng Biānmǎ：828573). Liánxì Diànhuà：42334464. Diànzǐ Yóuxiāng：zupct@opbedhvn.squares.cn

Sheng Sheng Zhao, Hao Cheng Square, 364 Zhi Han Road, Bama Yao Autonomous County, Hechi, Guangxi Autonomous Region. Postal Code: 828573. Phone Number：42334464. E-mail：zupct@opbedhvn.squares.cn

74。姓名: 卞冕祥

住址（公司）：广西壮族自治区桂林市临桂区游咚路 970 号勇院有限公司（邮政编码：138991）。联系电话：59488844。电子邮箱：qxpte@kahzcwie.biz.cn

Zhù zhǐ: Biàn Miǎn Xiáng Guǎngxī Zhuàngzú Zìzhìqū Guìlín Shì Lín Guì Qū Yóu Dōng Lù 970 Hào Yǒng Yuàn Yǒuxiàn Gōngsī (Yóuzhèng Biānmǎ：138991). Liánxì Diànhuà：59488844. Diànzǐ Yóuxiāng：qxpte@kahzcwie.biz.cn

Mian Xiang Bian, Yong Yuan Corporation, 970 You Dong Road, Lingui District, Guilin, Guangxi Autonomous Region. Postal Code: 138991. Phone Number：59488844. E-mail：qxpte@kahzcwie.biz.cn

75。姓名: 颜己勇

住址（医院）：广西壮族自治区柳州市柳城县葛近路 339 号可楚医院（邮政编码：791388）。联系电话：55074187。电子邮箱：cmatg@vsaytnuo.health.cn

Zhù zhǐ: Yán Jǐ Yǒng Guǎngxī Zhuàngzú Zìzhìqū Liǔzhōu Shì Liǔchéng Xiàn Gé Jìn Lù 339 Hào Kě Chǔ Yī Yuàn (Yóuzhèng Biānmǎ：791388). Liánxì Diànhuà：55074187. Diànzǐ Yóuxiāng：cmatg@vsaytnuo.health.cn

Ji Yong Yan, Ke Chu Hospital, 339 Ge Jin Road, Liucheng County, Liuzhou, Guangxi Autonomous Region. Postal Code: 791388. Phone Number：55074187. E-mail：cmatg@vsaytnuo.health.cn

76。姓名: 乐正晖坤

住址（机场）：广西壮族自治区贺州市富川瑶族自治县盛其路 270 号贺州冠辉国际机场（邮政编码：421828）。联系电话：12955835。电子邮箱：actow@pmtwhqzi.airports.cn

Zhù zhǐ: Yuèzhèng Huī Kūn Guǎngxī Zhuàngzú Zìzhìqū Hèzhōu Shì Fùchuān Yáozú Zìzhìxiàn Chéng Qí Lù 270 Hào Hèzōu Guān Huī Guó Jì Jī Chǎng (Yóuzhèng Biānmǎ：421828). Liánxì Diànhuà：12955835. Diànzǐ Yóuxiāng：actow@pmtwhqzi.airports.cn

Hui Kun Yuezheng, Hezhou Guan Hui International Airport, 270 Cheng Qi Road, Fuchuan Yao Autonomous County, Hezhou, Guangxi Autonomous Region. Postal Code: 421828. Phone Number：12955835. E-mail：actow@pmtwhqzi.airports.cn

77。姓名: 红岐铭

住址（火车站）：广西壮族自治区玉林市北流市隆发路 508 号玉林站（邮政编码：713094）。联系电话：86251746。电子邮箱：jfkep@eopvqcby.chr.cn

Zhù zhǐ: Hóng Qí Míng Guǎngxī Zhuàngzú Zìzhìqū Yùlín Shì Běi Liú Shì Lóng Fā Lù 508 Hào Yùlín Zhàn (Yóuzhèng Biānmǎ：713094). Liánxì Diànhuà：86251746. Diànzǐ Yóuxiāng：jfkep@eopvqcby.chr.cn

Qi Ming Hong, Yulin Railway Station, 508 Long Fa Road, Beiliu, Yulin, Guangxi Autonomous Region. Postal Code: 713094. Phone Number：86251746. E-mail：jfkep@eopvqcby.chr.cn

78。姓名: 田泽俊

住址（机场）：广西壮族自治区崇左市江州区昌启路 858 号崇左禹威国际机场（邮政编码：576613）。联系电话：27301507。电子邮箱：mupft@ctyegumb.airports.cn

Zhù zhǐ: Tián Zé Jùn Guǎngxī Zhuàngzú Zìzhìqū Chóng Zuǒ Shì Jiāng Zhōu Qū Chāng Qǐ Lù 858 Hào Cóng Zuǒ Yǔ Wēi Guó Jì Jī Chǎng (Yóuzhèng Biānmǎ：576613). Liánxì Diànhuà：27301507. Diànzǐ Yóuxiāng：mupft@ctyegumb.airports.cn

Ze Jun Tian, Chongzuo Yu Wei International Airport, 858 Chang Qi Road, Jiangzhou District, Chongzuo, Guangxi Autonomous Region. Postal Code: 576613. Phone Number：27301507. E-mail：mupft@ctyegumb.airports.cn

79。姓名: 钟强熔

住址（广场）：广西壮族自治区贵港市桂平市昌员路 951 号辙圣广场（邮政编码：212399）。联系电话：87635205。电子邮箱：
nuhei@epyznlfv.squares.cn

Zhù zhǐ: Zhōng Qiǎng Róng Guǎngxī Zhuàngzú Zìzhìqū Guìgǎng Shì Guìpíngshì Chāng Yún Lù 951 Hào Zhé Shèng Guǎng Chǎng (Yóuzhèng Biānmǎ：212399). Liánxì Diànhuà：87635205. Diànzǐ Yóuxiāng：nuhei@epyznlfv.squares.cn

Qiang Rong Zhong, Zhe Sheng Square, 951 Chang Yun Road, Guiping, Guigang, Guangxi Autonomous Region. Postal Code: 212399. Phone Number：87635205. E-mail：nuhei@epyznlfv.squares.cn

80。姓名: 危泽宽

住址（机场）：广西壮族自治区梧州市岑溪市民游路 687 号梧州辙桥国际机场（邮政编码：766497）。联系电话：57106597。电子邮箱：
zvifg@iolspkna.airports.cn

Zhù zhǐ: Wēi Zé Kuān Guǎngxī Zhuàngzú Zìzhìqū Wúzhōu Shì Cénxī Shì Mín Yóu Lù 687 Hào Wúzōu Zhé Qiáo Guó Jì Jī Chǎng (Yóuzhèng Biānmǎ：766497). Liánxì Diànhuà：57106597. Diànzǐ Yóuxiāng：zvifg@iolspkna.airports.cn

Ze Kuan Wei, Wuzhou Zhe Qiao International Airport, 687 Min You Road, Cenxi City, Wuzhou, Guangxi Autonomous Region. Postal Code: 766497. Phone Number：57106597. E-mail：zvifg@iolspkna.airports.cn

81。姓名: 贲浩星

住址（医院）：广西壮族自治区柳州市城中区食锤路 534 号茂圣医院（邮政编码：720492）。联系电话：14493276。电子邮箱：jicoh@xhweibgz.health.cn

Zhù zhǐ: Bēn Hào Xīng Guǎngxī Zhuàngzú Zìzhìqū Liǔzhōu Shì Chéngzhōng Qū Shí Chuí Lù 534 Hào Mào Shèng Yī Yuàn（Yóuzhèng Biānmǎ：720492). Liánxì Diànhuà：14493276. Diànzǐ Yóuxiāng：jicoh@xhweibgz.health.cn

Hao Xing Ben, Mao Sheng Hospital, 534 Shi Chui Road, Chengzhong District, Liuzhou, Guangxi Autonomous Region. Postal Code: 720492. Phone Number：14493276. E-mail：jicoh@xhweibgz.health.cn

82。姓名：夏侯翰发

住址（公园）：广西壮族自治区贵港市桂平市乐智路 438 号岐继公园（邮政编码：528390）。联系电话：78101194。电子邮箱：cpeyn@qtubjkdf.parks.cn

Zhù zhǐ: Xiàhóu Hàn Fā Guǎngxī Zhuàngzú Zìzhìqū Guìgǎng Shì Guìpíngshì Lè Zhì Lù 438 Hào Qí Jì Gōng Yuán（Yóuzhèng Biānmǎ：528390). Liánxì Diànhuà：78101194. Diànzǐ Yóuxiāng：cpeyn@qtubjkdf.parks.cn

Han Fa Xiahou, Qi Ji Park, 438 Le Zhi Road, Guiping, Guigang, Guangxi Autonomous Region. Postal Code: 528390. Phone Number：78101194. E-mail：cpeyn@qtubjkdf.parks.cn

83。姓名：关友尚

住址（医院）：广西壮族自治区来宾市武宣县鹤王路 327 号世浩医院（邮政编码：687356）。联系电话：57453976。电子邮箱：ksvwc@oldfkrjm.health.cn

Zhù zhǐ: Guān Yǒu Shàng Guǎngxī Zhuàngzú Zìzhìqū Láibīn Shì Wǔxuān Xiàn Hè Wàng Lù 327 Hào Shì Hào Yī Yuàn（Yóuzhèng Biānmǎ：687356). Liánxì Diànhuà：57453976. Diànzǐ Yóuxiāng：ksvwc@oldfkrjm.health.cn

You Shang Guan, Shi Hao Hospital, 327 He Wang Road, Wuxuan County, Laibin, Guangxi Autonomous Region. Postal Code: 687356. Phone Number：57453976. E-mail：ksvwc@oldfkrjm.health.cn

84。姓名: 司奎仲

住址（公司）：广西壮族自治区南宁市西乡塘区斌盛路 503 号宽独有限公司（邮政编码：858801）。联系电话：67013404。电子邮箱：knjre@pxkzotlw.biz.cn

Zhù zhǐ: Sī Kuí Zhòng Guǎngxī Zhuàngzú Zìzhìqū Nánníng Shì Xī Xiāng Táng Qū Bīn Shèng Lù 503 Hào Kuān Dú Yǒuxiàn Gōngsī (Yóuzhèng Biānmǎ：858801). Liánxì Diànhuà：67013404. Diànzǐ Yóuxiāng：knjre@pxkzotlw.biz.cn

Kui Zhong Si, Kuan Du Corporation, 503 Bin Sheng Road, Xixiangtang District, NanNing, Guangxi Autonomous Region. Postal Code: 858801. Phone Number：67013404. E-mail：knjre@pxkzotlw.biz.cn

85。姓名: 薛熔阳

住址（公司）：广西壮族自治区北海市铁山港区斌舟路 283 号福阳有限公司（邮政编码：499805）。联系电话：96405616。电子邮箱：rlykc@hpczlnid.biz.cn

Zhù zhǐ: Xuē Róng Yáng Guǎngxī Zhuàngzú Zìzhìqū Běihǎi Shì Tiě Shān Gǎng Qū Bīn Zhōu Lù 283 Hào Fú Yáng Yǒuxiàn Gōngsī (Yóuzhèng Biānmǎ：499805). Liánxì Diànhuà：96405616. Diànzǐ Yóuxiāng：rlykc@hpczlnid.biz.cn

Rong Yang Xue, Fu Yang Corporation, 283 Bin Zhou Road, Iron Mountain Port District, Beihai, Guangxi Autonomous Region. Postal Code: 499805. Phone Number：96405616. E-mail：rlykc@hpczlnid.biz.cn

86。姓名: 史波振

住址（广场）：广西壮族自治区玉林市容县己独路 808 号葆陆广场（邮政编码：975243）。联系电话：53187099。电子邮箱：qmfit@pdhxakrl.squares.cn

Zhù zhǐ: Shǐ Bō Zhèn Guǎngxī Zhuàngzú Zìzhìqū Yùlín Shì Róngxiàn Jǐ Dú Lù 808 Hào Bǎo Liù Guǎng Chǎng（Yóuzhèng Biānmǎ：975243）. Liánxì Diànhuà：53187099. Diànzǐ Yóuxiāng：qmfit@pdhxakrl.squares.cn

Bo Zhen Shi, Bao Liu Square, 808 Ji Du Road, Rong County, Yulin, Guangxi Autonomous Region. Postal Code: 975243. Phone Number：53187099. E-mail：qmfit@pdhxakrl.squares.cn

87。姓名: 糜亭学

住址（广场）：广西壮族自治区南宁市邕宁区民坚路 818 号员郁广场（邮政编码：677803）。联系电话：97475547。电子邮箱：aflxk@jraciedv.squares.cn

Zhù zhǐ: Mí Tíng Xué Guǎngxī Zhuàngzú Zìzhìqū Nánníng Shì Yōng Níng Qū Mín Jiān Lù 818 Hào Yún Yù Guǎng Chǎng（Yóuzhèng Biānmǎ：677803）. Liánxì Diànhuà：97475547. Diànzǐ Yóuxiāng：aflxk@jraciedv.squares.cn

Ting Xue Mi, Yun Yu Square, 818 Min Jian Road, Yongning District, NanNing, Guangxi Autonomous Region. Postal Code: 677803. Phone Number：97475547. E-mail：aflxk@jraciedv.squares.cn

88。姓名: 匡锤先

住址（机场）：广西壮族自治区南宁市江南区熔泽路 802 号南宁队不国际机场（邮政编码：621878）。联系电话：86949154。电子邮箱：cdobx@kxiltyaq.airports.cn

Zhù zhǐ: Kuāng Chuí Xiān Guǎngxī Zhuàngzú Zìzhìqū Nánníng Shì Jiāngnán Qū Róng Zé Lù 802 Hào Nánníng Duì Bù Guó Jì Jī Chǎng（Yóuzhèng Biānmǎ：621878）. Liánxì Diànhuà：86949154. Diànzǐ Yóuxiāng：cdobx@kxiltyaq.airports.cn

Chui Xian Kuang, NanNing Dui Bu International Airport, 802 Rong Ze Road, Gangnam District, NanNing, Guangxi Autonomous Region. Postal Code: 621878. Phone Number：86949154. E-mail：cdobx@kxiltyaq.airports.cn

89。姓名: 包宝化

住址（酒店）：广西壮族自治区柳州市柳南区汉绅路 325 号福龙酒店（邮政编码：522635）。联系电话：72824624。电子邮箱：oqkxi@xkoimqaz.biz.cn

Zhù zhǐ: Bāo Bǎo Huā Guǎngxī Zhuàngzú Zìzhìqū Liǔzhōu Shì Liǔ Nán Qū Hàn Shēn Lù 325 Hào Fú Lóng Jiǔ Diàn（Yóuzhèng Biānmǎ：522635). Liánxì Diànhuà：72824624. Diànzǐ Yóuxiāng：oqkxi@xkoimqaz.biz.cn

Bao Hua Bao, Fu Long Hotel, 325 Han Shen Road, Liunan District, Liuzhou, Guangxi Autonomous Region. Postal Code: 522635. Phone Number：72824624. E-mail：oqkxi@xkoimqaz.biz.cn

90。姓名: 公孙威咚

住址（酒店）：广西壮族自治区贵港市平南县浩晗路 263 号彬陆酒店（邮政编码：666815）。联系电话：85538139。电子邮箱：mozkx@porkseln.biz.cn

Zhù zhǐ: Gōngsūn Wēi Dōng Guǎngxī Zhuàngzú Zìzhìqū Guìgǎng Shì Píng Nán Xiàn Hào Hán Lù 263 Hào Bīn Lù Jiǔ Diàn（Yóuzhèng Biānmǎ：666815). Liánxì Diànhuà：85538139. Diànzǐ Yóuxiāng：mozkx@porkseln.biz.cn

Wei Dong Gongsun, Bin Lu Hotel, 263 Hao Han Road, Pingnan County, Guigang, Guangxi Autonomous Region. Postal Code: 666815. Phone Number：85538139. E-mail：mozkx@porkseln.biz.cn

CHAPTER 4: NAME, SURNAME & ADDRESSES (91-120)

91。姓名: 狄昌学

住址（火车站）：广西壮族自治区南宁市邕宁区洵王路 535 号南宁站（邮政编码：219822）。联系电话：78718094。电子邮箱：gszwf@sbjcdine.chr.cn

Zhù zhǐ: Dí Chāng Xué Guǎngxī Zhuàngzú Zìzhìqū Nánníng Shì Yōng Níng Qū Xún Wàng Lù 535 Hào Nánníng Zhàn（Yóuzhèng Biānmǎ：219822）. Liánxì Diànhuà: 78718094. Diànzǐ Yóuxiāng：gszwf@sbjcdine.chr.cn

Chang Xue Di, NanNing Railway Station, 535 Xun Wang Road, Yongning District, NanNing, Guangxi Autonomous Region. Postal Code: 219822. Phone Number：78718094. E-mail：gszwf@sbjcdine.chr.cn

92。姓名: 元大不

住址（酒店）：广西壮族自治区玉林市兴业县院豹路 809 号炯晖酒店（邮政编码：479350）。联系电话：74898544。电子邮箱：jylsi@zygwrnkx.biz.cn

Zhù zhǐ: Yuán Dài Bù Guǎngxī Zhuàngzú Zìzhìqū Yùlín Shì Xìngyè Xiàn Yuàn Bào Lù 809 Hào Jiǒng Huī Jiǔ Diàn（Yóuzhèng Biānmǎ：479350）. Liánxì Diànhuà：74898544. Diànzǐ Yóuxiāng：jylsi@zygwrnkx.biz.cn

Dai Bu Yuan, Jiong Hui Hotel, 809 Yuan Bao Road, Xingye County, Yulin, Guangxi Autonomous Region. Postal Code: 479350. Phone Number：74898544. E-mail：jylsi@zygwrnkx.biz.cn

93。姓名: 夔寰强

住址（机场）：广西壮族自治区来宾市合山市钊咚路 230 号来宾白发国际机场（邮政编码：795441）。联系电话：31973304。电子邮箱：hniwt@aqjecyns.airports.cn

Zhù zhǐ: Kuí Huán Qiáng Guǎngxī Zhuàngzú Zìzhìqū Láibīn Shì Hé Shān Shì Zhāo Dōng Lù 230 Hào Láibīn Bái Fā Guó Jì Jī Chǎng（Yóuzhèng Biānmǎ：795441）. Liánxì Diànhuà：31973304. Diànzǐ Yóuxiāng：hniwt@aqjecyns.airports.cn

Huan Qiang Kui, Laibin Bai Fa International Airport, 230 Zhao Dong Road, Heshan City, Laibin, Guangxi Autonomous Region. Postal Code: 795441. Phone Number：31973304. E-mail：hniwt@aqjecyns.airports.cn

94。姓名: 柯盛骥

住址（广场）：广西壮族自治区崇左市龙州县庆帆路 454 号汉歧广场（邮政编码：773024）。联系电话：53587072。电子邮箱：qmxol@dwqmlaux.squares.cn

Zhù zhǐ: Kē Chéng Jì Guǎngxī Zhuàngzú Zìzhìqū Chóng Zuǒ Shì Lóng Zhōu Xiàn Qìng Fān Lù 454 Hào Hàn Qí Guǎng Chǎng (Yóuzhèng Biānmǎ： 773024). Liánxì Diànhuà：53587072. Diànzǐ Yóuxiāng：qmxol@dwqmlaux.squares.cn

Cheng Ji Ke, Han Qi Square, 454 Qing Fan Road, Longzhou County, Chongzuo, Guangxi Autonomous Region. Postal Code: 773024. Phone Number：53587072. E-mail：qmxol@dwqmlaux.squares.cn

95。姓名: 钱屹国

住址（酒店）：广西壮族自治区崇左市宁明县彬易路 193 号沛强酒店（邮政编码：521960）。联系电话：39681424。电子邮箱：yqwbm@txcdmngz.biz.cn

Zhù zhǐ: Qián Yì Guó Guǎngxī Zhuàngzú Zìzhìqū Chóng Zuǒ Shì Níng Míng Xiàn Bīn Yì Lù 193 Hào Pèi Qiǎng Jiǔ Diàn (Yóuzhèng Biānmǎ： 521960). Liánxì Diànhuà：39681424. Diànzǐ Yóuxiāng：yqwbm@txcdmngz.biz.cn

Yi Guo Qian, Pei Qiang Hotel, 193 Bin Yi Road, Ningming County, Chongzuo, Guangxi Autonomous Region. Postal Code: 521960. Phone Number：39681424. E-mail：yqwbm@txcdmngz.biz.cn

96。姓名: 诸懂光

住址（广场）：广西壮族自治区北海市海城区乙葆路 983 号俊浩广场（邮政编码：498179）。联系电话：48508273。电子邮箱：qtide@jlbpchuw.squares.cn

Zhù zhǐ: Zhū Dǒng Guāng Guǎngxī Zhuàngzú Zìzhìqū Běihǎi Shì Hǎi Chéngqū Yǐ Bǎo Lù 983 Hào Jùn Hào Guǎng Chǎng（Yóuzhèng Biānmǎ：498179). Liánxì Diànhuà：48508273. Diànzǐ Yóuxiāng：qtide@jlbpchuw.squares.cn

Dong Guang Zhu, Jun Hao Square, 983 Yi Bao Road, Haicheng District, Beihai, Guangxi Autonomous Region. Postal Code: 498179. Phone Number：48508273. E-mail：qtide@jlbpchuw.squares.cn

97。姓名:通游队

住址（广场）：广西壮族自治区防城港市东兴市员成路 989 号昌敬广场（邮政编码：455715）。联系电话：23359935。电子邮箱：jbpsf@xbacupgm.squares.cn

Zhù zhǐ: Tōng Yóu Duì Guǎngxī Zhuàngzú Zìzhìqū Fángchénggǎng Shì Dōng Xīng Shì Yún Chéng Lù 989 Hào Chāng Jìng Guǎng Chǎng（Yóuzhèng Biānmǎ：455715). Liánxì Diànhuà：23359935. Diànzǐ Yóuxiāng：jbpsf@xbacupgm.squares.cn

You Dui Tong, Chang Jing Square, 989 Yun Cheng Road, Dongxing City, Fangchenggang, Guangxi Autonomous Region. Postal Code: 455715. Phone Number：23359935. E-mail：jbpsf@xbacupgm.squares.cn

98。姓名:杨钢守

住址（湖泊）：广西壮族自治区河池市宜州区陆员路 205 号迅冠湖（邮政编码：812711）。联系电话：52156983。电子邮箱：hjedr@nvksmdol.lakes.cn

Zhù zhǐ: Yáng Gāng Shǒu Guǎngxī Zhuàngzú Zìzhìqū Héchí Shì Yí zhōu qū Lù Yuán Lù 205 Hào Xùn Guān Hú（Yóuzhèng Biānmǎ：812711). Liánxì Diànhuà：52156983. Diànzǐ Yóuxiāng：hjedr@nvksmdol.lakes.cn

Gang Shou Yang, Xun Guan Lake, 205 Lu Yuan Road, Yizhou District, Hechi, Guangxi Autonomous Region. Postal Code: 812711. Phone Number：52156983. E-mail：hjedr@nvksmdol.lakes.cn

99。姓名: 崔嘉山

住址（公园）：广西壮族自治区柳州市柳北区郁计路 937 号超全公园（邮政编码：620532）。联系电话：83028065。电子邮箱：pcymg@ohxgwzus.parks.cn

Zhù zhǐ: Cuī Jiā Shān Guǎngxī Zhuàngzú Zìzhìqū Liǔzhōu Shì Liǔběi Qū Yù Jì Lù 937 Hào Chāo Quán Gōng Yuán（Yóuzhèng Biānmǎ：620532). Liánxì Diànhuà：83028065. Diànzǐ Yóuxiāng：pcymg@ohxgwzus.parks.cn

Jia Shan Cui, Chao Quan Park, 937 Yu Ji Road, Liubei District, Liuzhou, Guangxi Autonomous Region. Postal Code: 620532. Phone Number：83028065. E-mail：pcymg@ohxgwzus.parks.cn

100。姓名: 褚锤继

住址（大学）：广西壮族自治区贺州市钟山县威锤大学居不路 776 号（邮政编码：443611）。联系电话：43588565。电子邮箱：ngbfm@xaktvpqj.edu.cn

Zhù zhǐ: Chǔ Chuí Jì Guǎngxī Zhuàngzú Zìzhìqū Hèzhōu Shì Zhōng Shān Xiàn Wēi Chuí DàxuéJū Bù Lù 776 Hào（Yóuzhèng Biānmǎ：443611). Liánxì Diànhuà：43588565. Diànzǐ Yóuxiāng：ngbfm@xaktvpqj.edu.cn

Chui Ji Chu, Wei Chui University, 776 Ju Bu Road, Zhongshan County, Hezhou, Guangxi Autonomous Region. Postal Code: 443611. Phone Number：43588565. E-mail：ngbfm@xaktvpqj.edu.cn

101。姓名: 夏侯伦顺

住址（家庭）：广西壮族自治区南宁市良庆区郁福路 743 号顺腾公寓 9 层 978 室（邮政编码：186846）。联系电话：48654207。电子邮箱：kxbhd@rfehnlau.cn

Zhù zhǐ: Xiàhóu Lún Shùn Guǎngxī Zhuàngzú Zìzhìqū Nánníng Shì Liáng Qìng Qū Yù Fú Lù 743 Hào Shùn Téng Gōng Yù 9 Céng 978 Shì (Yóuzhèng Biānmǎ：186846). Liánxì Diànhuà：48654207. Diànzǐ Yóuxiāng：kxbhd@rfehnlau.cn

Lun Shun Xiahou, Room# 978, Floor# 9, Shun Teng Apartment, 743 Yu Fu Road, Liangqing District, NanNing, Guangxi Autonomous Region. Postal Code: 186846. Phone Number：48654207. E-mail：kxbhd@rfehnlau.cn

102。姓名: 司空泽钢

住址（广场）：广西壮族自治区钦州市钦北区珂风路 936 号绅秀广场（邮政编码：123575）。联系电话：30575379。电子邮箱：qbseu@aiqhfork.squares.cn

Zhù zhǐ: Sīkōng Zé Gāng Guǎngxī Zhuàngzú Zìzhìqū Qīnzhōu Shì Qīn Běi Qū Kē Fēng Lù 936 Hào Shēn Xiù Guǎng Chǎng (Yóuzhèng Biānmǎ：123575). Liánxì Diànhuà：30575379. Diànzǐ Yóuxiāng：qbseu@aiqhfork.squares.cn

Ze Gang Sikong, Shen Xiu Square, 936 Ke Feng Road, Qinbei District, Qinzhou, Guangxi Autonomous Region. Postal Code: 123575. Phone Number：30575379. E-mail：qbseu@aiqhfork.squares.cn

103。姓名: 蒯译茂

住址（家庭）：广西壮族自治区钦州市灵山县乙焯路 364 号秀钊公寓 46 层 496 室（邮政编码：910890）。联系电话：31413898。电子邮箱：wdjri@bltjunye.cn

Zhù zhǐ: Kuǎi Yì Mào Guǎngxī Zhuàngzú Zìzhìqū Qīnzhōu Shì Língshān Xiàn Yǐ Zhuō Lù 364 Hào Xiù Zhāo Gōng Yù 46 Céng 496 Shì (Yóuzhèng Biānmǎ：910890). Liánxì Diànhuà：31413898. Diànzǐ Yóuxiāng：wdjri@bltjunye.cn

Yi Mao Kuai, Room# 496, Floor# 46, Xiu Zhao Apartment, 364 Yi Zhuo Road, Lingshan County, Qinzhou, Guangxi Autonomous Region. Postal Code: 910890. Phone Number：31413898. E-mail：wdjri@bltjunye.cn

104。姓名: 诸郁成

住址（火车站）：广西壮族自治区柳州市柳北区继光路 476 号柳州站（邮政编码：869283）。联系电话：61728556。电子邮箱：qvogm@nsiglroa.chr.cn

Zhù zhǐ: Zhū Yù Chéng Guǎngxī Zhuàngzú Zìzhìqū Liǔzhōu Shì Liǔběi Qū Jì Guāng Lù 476 Hào Liǔzōu Zhàn（Yóuzhèng Biānmǎ：869283）. Liánxì Diànhuà：61728556. Diànzǐ Yóuxiāng：qvogm@nsiglroa.chr.cn

Yu Cheng Zhu, Liuzhou Railway Station, 476 Ji Guang Road, Liubei District, Liuzhou, Guangxi Autonomous Region. Postal Code: 869283. Phone Number：61728556. E-mail：qvogm@nsiglroa.chr.cn

105。姓名: 邓院际

住址（火车站）：广西壮族自治区崇左市天等县胜智路 746 号崇左站（邮政编码：875648）。联系电话：48080772。电子邮箱：rjqbi@wmtqjglk.chr.cn

Zhù zhǐ: Dèng Yuàn Jì Guǎngxī Zhuàngzú Zìzhìqū Chóng Zuǒ Shì Tiān Děng Xiàn Shēng Zhì Lù 746 Hào Cóng Zuǒ Zhàn（Yóuzhèng Biānmǎ：875648）. Liánxì Diànhuà：48080772. Diànzǐ Yóuxiāng：rjqbi@wmtqjglk.chr.cn

Yuan Ji Deng, Chongzuo Railway Station, 746 Sheng Zhi Road, Tiandeng County, Chongzuo, Guangxi Autonomous Region. Postal Code: 875648. Phone Number：48080772. E-mail：rjqbi@wmtqjglk.chr.cn

106。姓名: 班民福

住址（寺庙）：广西壮族自治区百色市田东县焯勇路 139 号游光寺（邮政编码：394005）。联系电话：92855098。电子邮箱：uomnp@arwovjil.god.cn

Zhù zhǐ: Bān Mín Fú Guǎngxī Zhuàngzú Zìzhìqū Bǎisè Shì Tián Dōng Xiàn Zhuō Yǒng Lù 139 Hào Yóu Guāng Sì（Yóuzhèng Biānmǎ：394005）. Liánxì Diànhuà：92855098. Diànzǐ Yóuxiāng：uomnp@arwovjil.god.cn

Min Fu Ban, You Guang Temple, 139 Zhuo Yong Road, Tiandong County, Baise, Guangxi Autonomous Region. Postal Code: 394005. Phone Number：92855098. E-mail：uomnp@arwovjil.god.cn

107。姓名: 拓跋汉风

住址（家庭）：广西壮族自治区柳州市融水苗族自治县化沛路 204 号甫科公寓 2 层 386 室（邮政编码：958279）。联系电话：85772179。电子邮箱：inkcs@gktmjois.cn

Zhù zhǐ: Tuòbá Hàn Fēng Guǎngxī Zhuàngzú Zìzhìqū Liǔzhōu Shì Róng Shuǐ Miáozú Zìzhìxiàn Huā Pèi Lù 204 Hào Fǔ Kē Gōng Yù 2 Céng 386 Shì (Yóuzhèng Biānmǎ: 958279). Liánxì Diànhuà：85772179. Diànzǐ Yóuxiāng：inkcs@gktmjois.cn

Han Feng Tuoba, Room# 386, Floor# 2, Fu Ke Apartment, 204 Hua Pei Road, Rongshui Miao Autonomous County, Liuzhou, Guangxi Autonomous Region. Postal Code: 958279. Phone Number：85772179. E-mail：inkcs@gktmjois.cn

108。姓名: 归维茂

住址（医院）：广西壮族自治区河池市宜州区泽国路 791 号仲胜医院（邮政编码：338270）。联系电话：44421611。电子邮箱：wdzqa@ixnmprfl.health.cn

Zhù zhǐ: Guī Wéi Mào Guǎngxī Zhuàngzú Zìzhìqū Héchí Shì Yí zhōu qū Zé Guó Lù 791 Hào Zhòng Shēng Yī Yuàn (Yóuzhèng Biānmǎ: 338270). Liánxì Diànhuà: 44421611. Diànzǐ Yóuxiāng：wdzqa@ixnmprfl.health.cn

Wei Mao Gui, Zhong Sheng Hospital, 791 Ze Guo Road, Yizhou District, Hechi, Guangxi Autonomous Region. Postal Code: 338270. Phone Number：44421611. E-mail：wdzqa@ixnmprfl.health.cn

109。姓名: 柯晗浩

住址（广场）：广西壮族自治区防城港市港口区舟翼路 282 号洵山广场（邮政编码：598432）。联系电话：18046674。电子邮箱：ozdsr@mfjckegb.squares.cn

Zhù zhǐ: Kē Hán Hào Guǎngxī Zhuàngzú Zìzhìqū Fángchénggǎng Shì Gǎngkǒu Qū Zhōu Yì Lù 282 Hào Xún Shān Guǎng Chǎng (Yóuzhèng Biānmǎ：598432). Liánxì Diànhuà：18046674. Diànzǐ Yóuxiāng：ozdsr@mfjckegb.squares.cn

Han Hao Ke, Xun Shan Square, 282 Zhou Yi Road, Port Area, Fangchenggang, Guangxi Autonomous Region. Postal Code: 598432. Phone Number：18046674. E-mail：ozdsr@mfjckegb.squares.cn

110。姓名: 双队强

住址（火车站）：广西壮族自治区百色市德保县泽来路 864 号百色站（邮政编码：725823）。联系电话：28491308。电子邮箱：gtzhu@xquypzng.chr.cn

Zhù zhǐ: Shuāng Duì Qiáng Guǎngxī Zhuàngzú Zìzhìqū Bǎisè Shì Dé Bǎo Xiàn Zé Lái Lù 864 Hào Bǎisè Zhàn (Yóuzhèng Biānmǎ：725823). Liánxì Diànhuà：28491308. Diànzǐ Yóuxiāng：gtzhu@xquypzng.chr.cn

Dui Qiang Shuang, Baise Railway Station, 864 Ze Lai Road, Debao County, Baise, Guangxi Autonomous Region. Postal Code: 725823. Phone Number：28491308. E-mail：gtzhu@xquypzng.chr.cn

111。姓名: 何冠风

住址（酒店）：广西壮族自治区钦州市灵山县化钊路 401 号克启酒店（邮政编码：840131）。联系电话：89597728。电子邮箱：vlwns@mjqpaxfe.biz.cn

Zhù zhǐ: Hé Guàn Fēng Guǎngxī Zhuàngzú Zìzhìqū Qīnzhōu Shì Língshān Xiàn Huā Zhāo Lù 401 Hào Kè Qǐ Jiǔ Diàn (Yóuzhèng Biānmǎ：840131). Liánxì Diànhuà：89597728. Diànzǐ Yóuxiāng：vlwns@mjqpaxfe.biz.cn

Guan Feng He, Ke Qi Hotel, 401 Hua Zhao Road, Lingshan County, Qinzhou, Guangxi Autonomous Region. Postal Code: 840131. Phone Number：89597728. E-mail：vlwns@mjqpaxfe.biz.cn

112。姓名: 强汉金

住址（大学）：广西壮族自治区玉林市陆川县泽阳大学维焯路 918 号（邮政编码：865469）。联系电话：42014127。电子邮箱：hubnc@ojsvpxwi.edu.cn

Zhù zhǐ: Qiáng Hàn Jīn Guǎngxī Zhuàngzú Zìzhìqū Yùlín Shì Lù Chuān Xiàn Zé Yáng DàxuéWéi Chāo Lù 918 Hào (Yóuzhèng Biānmǎ：865469). Liánxì Diànhuà：42014127. Diànzǐ Yóuxiāng：hubnc@ojsvpxwi.edu.cn

Han Jin Qiang, Ze Yang University, 918 Wei Chao Road, Luchuan County, Yulin, Guangxi Autonomous Region. Postal Code: 865469. Phone Number：42014127. E-mail：hubnc@ojsvpxwi.edu.cn

113。姓名: 红原桥

住址（火车站）：广西壮族自治区北海市海城区浩敬路 960 号北海站（邮政编码：943803）。联系电话：81653560。电子邮箱：sjpyz@linzkghu.chr.cn

Zhù zhǐ: Hóng Yuán Qiáo Guǎngxī Zhuàngzú Zìzhìqū Běihǎi Shì Hǎi Chéngqū Hào Jìng Lù 960 Hào Běiǎi Zhàn (Yóuzhèng Biānmǎ：943803). Liánxì Diànhuà：81653560. Diànzǐ Yóuxiāng：sjpyz@linzkghu.chr.cn

Yuan Qiao Hong, Beihai Railway Station, 960 Hao Jing Road, Haicheng District, Beihai, Guangxi Autonomous Region. Postal Code: 943803. Phone Number：81653560. E-mail：sjpyz@linzkghu.chr.cn

114。姓名: 熊舟亭

住址（湖泊）：广西壮族自治区崇左市天等县化懂路 416 号泽陶湖（邮政编码：325782）。联系电话：66622115。电子邮箱：slwyt@mthsfigw.lakes.cn

Zhù zhǐ: Xióng Zhōu Tíng Guǎngxī Zhuàngzú Zìzhìqū Chóng Zuǒ Shì Tiān Děng Xiàn Huà Dǒng Lù 416 Hào Zé Táo Hú (Yóuzhèng Biānmǎ： 325782). Liánxì Diànhuà： 66622115. Diànzǐ Yóuxiāng：slwyt@mthsfigw.lakes.cn

Zhou Ting Xiong, Ze Tao Lake, 416 Hua Dong Road, Tiandeng County, Chongzuo, Guangxi Autonomous Region. Postal Code: 325782. Phone Number： 66622115. E-mail：slwyt@mthsfigw.lakes.cn

115。姓名: 荀德钢

住址（博物院）：广西壮族自治区防城港市东兴市译龙路 428 号防城港博物馆（邮政编码：986489）。联系电话：25269123。电子邮箱：lojpn@pnhgskfr.museums.cn

Zhù zhǐ: Xún Dé Gāng Guǎngxī Zhuàngzú Zìzhìqū Fángchénggǎng Shì Dōng Xīng Shì Yì Lóng Lù 428 Hào Fángcénggǎng Bó Wù Guǎn (Yóuzhèng Biānmǎ： 986489). Liánxì Diànhuà： 25269123. Diànzǐ Yóuxiāng：lojpn@pnhgskfr.museums.cn

De Gang Xun, Fangchenggang Museum, 428 Yi Long Road, Dongxing City, Fangchenggang, Guangxi Autonomous Region. Postal Code: 986489. Phone Number： 25269123. E-mail：lojpn@pnhgskfr.museums.cn

116。姓名: 苏庆惟

住址（湖泊）：广西壮族自治区桂林市灵川县先陆路 745 号易斌湖（邮政编码：986510）。联系电话：83704046。电子邮箱：ozjgm@qktzmovr.lakes.cn

Zhù zhǐ: Sū Qìng Wéi Guǎngxī Zhuàngzú Zìzhìqū Guìlín Shì Líng Chuānxiàn Xiān Liù Lù 745 Hào Yì Bīn Hú (Yóuzhèng Biānmǎ： 986510). Liánxì Diànhuà： 83704046. Diànzǐ Yóuxiāng：ozjgm@qktzmovr.lakes.cn

Qing Wei Su, Yi Bin Lake, 745 Xian Liu Road, Lingchuan County, Guilin, Guangxi Autonomous Region. Postal Code: 986510. Phone Number： 83704046. E-mail：ozjgm@qktzmovr.lakes.cn

117。姓名: 夏侯大庆

住址（寺庙）：广西壮族自治区玉林市北流市先惟路 568 号星庆寺（邮政编码：373954）。联系电话：61208715。电子邮箱：giflp@fiohnpgm.god.cn

Zhù zhǐ: Xiàhóu Dài Qìng Guǎngxī Zhuàngzú Zìzhìqū Yùlín Shì Běi Liú Shì Xiān Wéi Lù 568 Hào Xīng Qìng Sì (Yóuzhèng Biānmǎ：373954). Liánxì Diànhuà：61208715. Diànzǐ Yóuxiāng：giflp@fiohnpgm.god.cn

Dai Qing Xiahou, Xing Qing Temple, 568 Xian Wei Road, Beiliu, Yulin, Guangxi Autonomous Region. Postal Code: 373954. Phone Number：61208715. E-mail：giflp@fiohnpgm.god.cn

118。姓名: 祖中智

住址（广场）：广西壮族自治区梧州市龙圩区辙乙路 274 号冠克广场（邮政编码：893280）。联系电话：72878582。电子邮箱：ryiaq@lsmoekyf.squares.cn

Zhù zhǐ: Zǔ Zhòng Zhì Guǎngxī Zhuàngzú Zìzhìqū Wúzhōu Shì Lóng Wéi Qū Zhé Yǐ Lù 274 Hào Guān Kè Guǎng Chǎng (Yóuzhèng Biānmǎ：893280). Liánxì Diànhuà：72878582. Diànzǐ Yóuxiāng：ryiaq@lsmoekyf.squares.cn

Zhong Zhi Zu, Guan Ke Square, 274 Zhe Yi Road, Longxu District, Wuzhou, Guangxi Autonomous Region. Postal Code: 893280. Phone Number：72878582. E-mail：ryiaq@lsmoekyf.squares.cn

119。姓名: 桂冠晖

住址（公司）：广西壮族自治区梧州市藤县威珏路 588 号屹焯有限公司（邮政编码：680823）。联系电话：15126421。电子邮箱：xgpfi@slprnkih.biz.cn

Zhù zhǐ: Guì Guān Huī Guǎngxī Zhuàngzú Zìzhìqū Wúzhōu Shì Téng Xiàn Wēi Jué Lù 588 Hào Yì Chāo Yǒuxiàn Gōngsī (Yóuzhèng Biānmǎ：680823). Liánxì Diànhuà：15126421. Diànzǐ Yóuxiāng：xgpfi@slprnkih.biz.cn

Guan Hui Gui, Yi Chao Corporation, 588 Wei Jue Road, Fuji County, Wuzhou, Guangxi Autonomous Region. Postal Code: 680823. Phone Number：15126421. E-mail：xgpfi@slprnkih.biz.cn

120。姓名: 蓬亭舟

住址（酒店）：广西壮族自治区百色市田阳区威仲路 523 号征强酒店（邮政编码：130559）。联系电话：36037402。电子邮箱：baofc@vwmxndub.biz.cn

Zhù zhǐ: Péng Tíng Zhōu Guǎngxī Zhuàngzú Zìzhìqū Bǎisè Shì Tiányáng Qū Wēi Zhòng Lù 523 Hào Zhēng Qiáng Jiǔ Diàn（Yóuzhèng Biānmǎ：130559). Liánxì Diànhuà：36037402. Diànzǐ Yóuxiāng：baofc@vwmxndub.biz.cn

Ting Zhou Peng, Zheng Qiang Hotel, 523 Wei Zhong Road, Tianyang District, Baise, Guangxi Autonomous Region. Postal Code: 130559. Phone Number：36037402. E-mail：baofc@vwmxndub.biz.cn

CHAPTER 5: NAME, SURNAME & ADDRESSES (121-150)

121。姓名: 韶译风

住址（大学）：广西壮族自治区梧州市藤县帆成大学全石路 604 号（邮政编码：929037）。联系电话：72890551。电子邮箱：agwxy@pambqhlu.edu.cn

Zhù zhǐ: Sháo Yì Fēng Guǎngxī Zhuàngzú Zìzhìqū Wúzhōu Shì Téng Xiàn Fān Chéng DàxuéQuán Shí Lù 604 Hào (Yóuzhèng Biānmǎ：929037). Liánxì Diànhuà：72890551. Diànzǐ Yóuxiāng：agwxy@pambqhlu.edu.cn

Yi Feng Shao, Fan Cheng University, 604 Quan Shi Road, Fuji County, Wuzhou, Guangxi Autonomous Region. Postal Code: 929037. Phone Number：72890551. E-mail：agwxy@pambqhlu.edu.cn

122。姓名: 陈征跃

住址（火车站）：广西壮族自治区来宾市象州县民愈路 101 号来宾站（邮政编码：885193）。联系电话：66934088。电子邮箱：jpicr@ofldxeih.chr.cn

Zhù zhǐ: Chén Zhēng Yuè Guǎngxī Zhuàngzú Zìzhìqū Láibīn Shì Xiàng Zhōu Xiàn Mín Yù Lù 101 Hào Láibīn Zhàn (Yóuzhèng Biānmǎ：885193). Liánxì Diànhuà：66934088. Diànzǐ Yóuxiāng：jpicr@ofldxeih.chr.cn

Zheng Yue Chen, Laibin Railway Station, 101 Min Yu Road, Xiangzhou County, Laibin, Guangxi Autonomous Region. Postal Code: 885193. Phone Number：66934088. E-mail：jpicr@ofldxeih.chr.cn

123。姓名: 贝沛屹

住址（公共汽车站）：广西壮族自治区梧州市藤县珏智路 573 号坚彬站（邮政编码：770812）。联系电话：42320253。电子邮箱：ctepi@tsnbgzru.transport.cn

Zhù zhǐ: Bèi Bèi Yì Guǎngxī Zhuàngzú Zìzhìqū Wúzhōu Shì Téng Xiàn Jué Zhì Lù 573 Hào Jiān Bīn Zhàn (Yóuzhèng Biānmǎ：770812). Liánxì Diànhuà：42320253. Diànzǐ Yóuxiāng：ctepi@tsnbgzru.transport.cn

Bei Yi Bei, Jian Bin Bus Station, 573 Jue Zhi Road, Fuji County, Wuzhou, Guangxi Autonomous Region. Postal Code: 770812. Phone Number：42320253. E-mail：ctepi@tsnbgzru.transport.cn

124。姓名: 师顺可

住址（家庭）：广西壮族自治区来宾市合山市陶院路 320 号刚人公寓 6 层 872 室（邮政编码：774959）。联系电话：82293870。电子邮箱：acinj@guymtwpa.cn

Zhù zhǐ: Shī Shùn Kě Guǎngxī Zhuàngzú Zìzhìqū Láibīn Shì Hé Shān Shì Táo Yuàn Lù 320 Hào Gāng Rén Gōng Yù 6 Céng 872 Shì (Yóuzhèng Biānmǎ：774959). Liánxì Diànhuà：82293870. Diànzǐ Yóuxiāng：acinj@guymtwpa.cn

Shun Ke Shi, Room# 872, Floor# 6, Gang Ren Apartment, 320 Tao Yuan Road, Heshan City, Laibin, Guangxi Autonomous Region. Postal Code: 774959. Phone Number：82293870. E-mail：acinj@guymtwpa.cn

125。姓名: 弓泽队

住址（医院）：广西壮族自治区贺州市钟山县跃桥路 807 号黎土医院（邮政编码：683426）。联系电话：80265552。电子邮箱：xhjbi@gdrnkiqt.health.cn

Zhù zhǐ: Gōng Zé Duì Guǎngxī Zhuàngzú Zìzhìqū Hèzhōu Shì Zhōng Shān Xiàn Yuè Qiáo Lù 807 Hào Lí Tǔ Yī Yuàn (Yóuzhèng Biānmǎ：683426). Liánxì Diànhuà：80265552. Diànzǐ Yóuxiāng：xhjbi@gdrnkiqt.health.cn

Ze Dui Gong, Li Tu Hospital, 807 Yue Qiao Road, Zhongshan County, Hezhou, Guangxi Autonomous Region. Postal Code: 683426. Phone Number：80265552. E-mail：xhjbi@gdrnkiqt.health.cn

126。姓名: 史汉隆

住址（家庭）：广西壮族自治区崇左市扶绥县茂磊路 516 号不楚公寓 46 层 811 室（邮政编码：638245）。联系电话：34740288。电子邮箱：awtgo@clxwfmhj.cn

Zhù zhǐ: Shǐ Hàn Lóng Guǎngxī Zhuàngzú Zìzhìqū Chóng Zuǒ Shì Fú Suí Xiàn Mào Lěi Lù 516 Hào Bù Chǔ Gōng Yù 46 Céng 811 Shì (Yóuzhèng Biānmǎ：638245). Liánxì Diànhuà：34740288. Diànzǐ Yóuxiāng：awtgo@clxwfmhj.cn

Han Long Shi, Room# 811, Floor# 46, Bu Chu Apartment, 516 Mao Lei Road, Fusui County, Chongzuo, Guangxi Autonomous Region. Postal Code: 638245. Phone Number：34740288. E-mail：awtgo@clxwfmhj.cn

127。姓名: 宦帆澜

住址（家庭）：广西壮族自治区梧州市蒙山县泽可路 404 号辙原公寓 6 层 643 室（邮政编码：694139）。联系电话：55413508。电子邮箱：jreat@ucdlfwvy.cn

Zhù zhǐ: Huàn Fān Lán Guǎngxī Zhuàngzú Zìzhìqū Wúzhōu Shì Méng Shānxiàn Zé Kě Lù 404 Hào Zhé Yuán Gōng Yù 6 Céng 643 Shì (Yóuzhèng Biānmǎ：694139). Liánxì Diànhuà：55413508. Diànzǐ Yóuxiāng：jreat@ucdlfwvy.cn

Fan Lan Huan, Room# 643, Floor# 6, Zhe Yuan Apartment, 404 Ze Ke Road, Mengshan County, Wuzhou, Guangxi Autonomous Region. Postal Code: 694139. Phone Number：55413508. E-mail：jreat@ucdlfwvy.cn

128。姓名: 鱼启锡

住址（公司）：广西壮族自治区南宁市横州市顺易路 961 号亭维有限公司（邮政编码：306558）。联系电话：42301961。电子邮箱：ncfrb@snicgtel.biz.cn

Zhù zhǐ: Yú Qǐ Xī Guǎngxī Zhuàngzú Zìzhìqū Nánníng Shì Héng Zhōu Shì Shùn Yì Lù 961 Hào Tíng Wéi Yǒuxiàn Gōngsī (Yóuzhèng Biānmǎ：306558). Liánxì Diànhuà：42301961. Diànzǐ Yóuxiāng：ncfrb@snicgtel.biz.cn

Qi Xi Yu, Ting Wei Corporation, 961 Shun Yi Road, Hengzhou, NanNing, Guangxi Autonomous Region. Postal Code: 306558. Phone Number：42301961. E-mail：ncfrb@snicgtel.biz.cn

129。姓名: 郑嘉嘉

住址（广场）：广西壮族自治区来宾市象州县淘汉路 697 号领沛广场（邮政编码：541076）。联系电话：67957844。电子邮箱：qjdhs@bnmxezpv.squares.cn

Zhù zhǐ: Zhèng Jiā Jiā Guǎngxī Zhuàngzú Zìzhìqū Láibīn Shì Xiàng Zhōu Xiàn Xún Hàn Lù 697 Hào Lǐng Pèi Guǎng Chǎng (Yóuzhèng Biānmǎ：541076). Liánxì Diànhuà：67957844. Diànzǐ Yóuxiāng：qjdhs@bnmxezpv.squares.cn

Jia Jia Zheng, Ling Pei Square, 697 Xun Han Road, Xiangzhou County, Laibin, Guangxi Autonomous Region. Postal Code: 541076. Phone Number：67957844. E-mail：qjdhs@bnmxezpv.squares.cn

130。姓名: 单石坤

住址（医院）：广西壮族自治区南宁市隆安县仓刚路 837 号进坡医院（邮政编码：774988）。联系电话：40902195。电子邮箱：nmdab@oksvjhlb.health.cn

Zhù zhǐ: Shàn Dàn Kūn Guǎngxī Zhuàngzú Zìzhìqū Nánníng Shì Lóngānxiàn Cāng Gāng Lù 837 Hào Jìn Pō Yī Yuàn (Yóuzhèng Biānmǎ：774988). Liánxì Diànhuà：40902195. Diànzǐ Yóuxiāng：nmdab@oksvjhlb.health.cn

Dan Kun Shan, Jin Po Hospital, 837 Cang Gang Road, Longan County, NanNing, Guangxi Autonomous Region. Postal Code: 774988. Phone Number：40902195. E-mail：nmdab@oksvjhlb.health.cn

131。姓名: 商威化

住址（公共汽车站）：广西壮族自治区贺州市昭平县甫先路 836 号星坚站（邮政编码：945581）。联系电话：51252835。电子邮箱：dlgpa@dvimckez.transport.cn

Zhù zhǐ: Shāng Wēi Huà Guǎngxī Zhuàngzú Zìzhìqū Hèzhōu Shì Zhāopíng Xiàn Fǔ Xiān Lù 836 Hào Xīng Jiān Zhàn（Yóuzhèng Biānmǎ：945581). Liánxì Diànhuà：51252835. Diànzǐ Yóuxiāng：dlgpa@dvimckez.transport.cn

Wei Hua Shang, Xing Jian Bus Station, 836 Fu Xian Road, Zhaoping County, Hezhou, Guangxi Autonomous Region. Postal Code: 945581. Phone Number：51252835. E-mail：dlgpa@dvimckez.transport.cn

132。姓名: 封冠计

住址（公共汽车站）：广西壮族自治区百色市德保县超阳路 723 号奎谢站（邮政编码：606768）。联系电话：94739930。电子邮箱：zvchs@idvzhjky.transport.cn

Zhù zhǐ: Fēng Guàn Jì Guǎngxī Zhuàngzú Zìzhìqū Bǎisè Shì Dé Bǎo Xiàn Chāo Yáng Lù 723 Hào Kuí Xiè Zhàn（Yóuzhèng Biānmǎ：606768). Liánxì Diànhuà：94739930. Diànzǐ Yóuxiāng：zvchs@idvzhjky.transport.cn

Guan Ji Feng, Kui Xie Bus Station, 723 Chao Yang Road, Debao County, Baise, Guangxi Autonomous Region. Postal Code: 606768. Phone Number：94739930. E-mail：zvchs@idvzhjky.transport.cn

133。姓名: 梅豹石

住址（医院）：广西壮族自治区北海市银海区郁人路 891 号民柱医院（邮政编码：872672）。联系电话：70677667。电子邮箱：towuy@xptzmnwe.health.cn

Zhù zhǐ: Méi Bào Shí Guǎngxī Zhuàngzú Zìzhìqū Běihǎi Shì Yín Hǎi Qū Yù Rén Lù 891 Hào Mín Zhù Yī Yuàn（Yóuzhèng Biānmǎ：872672). Liánxì Diànhuà：70677667. Diànzǐ Yóuxiāng：towuy@xptzmnwe.health.cn

Bao Shi Mei, Min Zhu Hospital, 891 Yu Ren Road, Yinhai District, Beihai, Guangxi Autonomous Region. Postal Code: 872672. Phone Number：70677667. E-mail：towuy@xptzmnwe.health.cn

134。姓名: 冯自石

住址（大学）：广西壮族自治区梧州市藤县顺红大学光骥路 641 号（邮政编码：724078）。联系电话：23585069。电子邮箱：ejxad@qnrdkxgw.edu.cn

Zhù zhǐ: Féng Zì Dàn Guǎngxī Zhuàngzú Zìzhìqū Wúzhōu Shì Téng Xiàn Shùn Hóng DàxuéGuāng Jì Lù 641 Hào（Yóuzhèng Biānmǎ：724078). Liánxì Diànhuà：23585069. Diànzǐ Yóuxiāng：ejxad@qnrdkxgw.edu.cn

Zi Dan Feng, Shun Hong University, 641 Guang Ji Road, Fuji County, Wuzhou, Guangxi Autonomous Region. Postal Code: 724078. Phone Number：23585069. E-mail：ejxad@qnrdkxgw.edu.cn

135。姓名: 平宽磊

住址（家庭）：广西壮族自治区南宁市兴宁区山铁路 959 号锤炯公寓 39 层 341 室（邮政编码：963281）。联系电话：63627072。电子邮箱：otcqx@hzsgntyp.cn

Zhù zhǐ: Píng Kuān Lěi Guǎngxī Zhuàngzú Zìzhìqū Nánníng Shì Xìng Níng Qū Shān Tiě Lù 959 Hào Chuí Jiǒng Gōng Yù 39 Céng 341 Shì (Yóuzhèng Biānmǎ：963281). Liánxì Diànhuà：63627072. Diànzǐ Yóuxiāng：otcqx@hzsgntyp.cn

Kuan Lei Ping, Room# 341, Floor# 39, Chui Jiong Apartment, 959 Shan Tie Road, Xingning District, NanNing, Guangxi Autonomous Region. Postal Code: 963281. Phone Number：63627072. E-mail：otcqx@hzsgntyp.cn

136。姓名: 水风队

住址（酒店）：广西壮族自治区崇左市大新县其大路 706 号振易酒店（邮政编码：314099）。联系电话：30619890。电子邮箱：xlraw@cdzriyst.biz.cn

Zhù zhǐ: Shuǐ Fēng Duì Guǎngxī Zhuàngzú Zìzhìqū Chóng Zuǒ Shì Dà Xīn Xiàn Qí Dài Lù 706 Hào Zhèn Yì Jiǔ Diàn (Yóuzhèng Biānmǎ: 314099). Liánxì Diànhuà: 30619890. Diànzǐ Yóuxiāng: xlraw@cdzriyst.biz.cn

Feng Dui Shui, Zhen Yi Hotel, 706 Qi Dai Road, Daxin County, Chongzuo, Guangxi Autonomous Region. Postal Code: 314099. Phone Number: 30619890. E-mail: xlraw@cdzriyst.biz.cn

137。姓名: 邴咚谢

住址（机场）：广西壮族自治区桂林市永福县其风路 485 号桂林兵振国际机场（邮政编码：363312）。联系电话：27070568。电子邮箱：xuost@amlicqfu.airports.cn

Zhù zhǐ: Bǐng Dōng Xiè Guǎngxī Zhuàngzú Zìzhìqū Guìlín Shì Yǒngfú Xiàn Qí Fēng Lù 485 Hào Gulín Bīng Zhèn Guó Jì Jī Chǎng (Yóuzhèng Biānmǎ: 363312). Liánxì Diànhuà: 27070568. Diànzǐ Yóuxiāng: xuost@amlicqfu.airports.cn

Dong Xie Bing, Guilin Bing Zhen International Airport, 485 Qi Feng Road, Yongfu County, Guilin, Guangxi Autonomous Region. Postal Code: 363312. Phone Number: 27070568. E-mail: xuost@amlicqfu.airports.cn

138。姓名: 牧辉不

住址（博物院）：广西壮族自治区北海市合浦县守南路 619 号北海博物馆（邮政编码：867531）。联系电话：19639568。电子邮箱：frisn@edahyofc.museums.cn

Zhù zhǐ: Mù Huī Bù Guǎngxī Zhuàngzú Zìzhìqū Běihǎi Shì Hépǔ Xiàn Shǒu Nán Lù 619 Hào Běiǎi Bó Wù Guǎn (Yóuzhèng Biānmǎ: 867531). Liánxì Diànhuà: 19639568. Diànzǐ Yóuxiāng: frisn@edahyofc.museums.cn

Hui Bu Mu, Beihai Museum, 619 Shou Nan Road, Hepu County, Beihai, Guangxi Autonomous Region. Postal Code: 867531. Phone Number: 19639568. E-mail: frisn@edahyofc.museums.cn

139。姓名: 越谢浩

住址（医院）：广西壮族自治区河池市南丹县庆绅路 197 号克兵医院（邮政编码：422547）。联系电话：26074633。电子邮箱：oyiwe@oufkvqix.health.cn

Zhù zhǐ: Yuè Xiè Hào Guǎngxī Zhuàngzú Zìzhìqū Héchí Shì Nán Dān Xiàn Qìng Shēn Lù 197 Hào Kè Bīng Yī Yuàn（Yóuzhèng Biānmǎ：422547). Liánxì Diànhuà：26074633. Diànzǐ Yóuxiāng：oyiwe@oufkvqix.health.cn

Xie Hao Yue, Ke Bing Hospital, 197 Qing Shen Road, Nandan County, Hechi, Guangxi Autonomous Region. Postal Code: 422547. Phone Number：26074633. E-mail：oyiwe@oufkvqix.health.cn

140。姓名: 谷祥全

住址（寺庙）：广西壮族自治区柳州市融水苗族自治县葆近路 623 号仓亚寺（邮政编码：565656）。联系电话：41914225。电子邮箱：dfgle@tloechya.god.cn

Zhù zhǐ: Gǔ Xiáng Quán Guǎngxī Zhuàngzú Zìzhìqū Liǔzhōu Shì Róng Shuǐ Miáozú Zìzhìxiàn Bǎo Jìn Lù 623 Hào Cāng Yà Sì（Yóuzhèng Biānmǎ：565656). Liánxì Diànhuà：41914225. Diànzǐ Yóuxiāng：dfgle@tloechya.god.cn

Xiang Quan Gu, Cang Ya Temple, 623 Bao Jin Road, Rongshui Miao Autonomous County, Liuzhou, Guangxi Autonomous Region. Postal Code: 565656. Phone Number：41914225. E-mail：dfgle@tloechya.god.cn

141。姓名: 章惟黎

住址（酒店）：广西壮族自治区梧州市岑溪市源山路 188 号亭豪酒店（邮政编码：576630）。联系电话：63111564。电子邮箱：zmkhw@rscfyulm.biz.cn

Zhù zhǐ: Zhāng Wéi Lí Guǎngxī Zhuàngzú Zìzhìqū Wúzhōu Shì Cénxī Shì Yuán Shān Lù 188 Hào Tíng Háo Jiǔ Diàn（Yóuzhèng Biānmǎ：576630). Liánxì Diànhuà：63111564. Diànzǐ Yóuxiāng：zmkhw@rscfyulm.biz.cn

Wei Li Zhang, Ting Hao Hotel, 188 Yuan Shan Road, Cenxi City, Wuzhou, Guangxi Autonomous Region. Postal Code: 576630. Phone Number：63111564. E-mail：zmkhw@rscfyulm.biz.cn

142。姓名: 殳寰翰

住址（医院）：广西壮族自治区防城港市上思县陆沛路 166 号歧禹医院（邮政编码：159073）。联系电话：90315971。电子邮箱：zigqj@hcywbaen.health.cn

Zhù zhǐ: Shū Huán Hàn Guǎngxī Zhuàngzú Zìzhìqū Fángchénggǎng Shì Shàng Sī Xiàn Liù Bèi Lù 166 Hào Qí Yǔ Yī Yuàn (Yóuzhèng Biānmǎ：159073). Liánxì Diànhuà：90315971. Diànzǐ Yóuxiāng：zigqj@hcywbaen.health.cn

Huan Han Shu, Qi Yu Hospital, 166 Liu Bei Road, Shangsi County, Fangchenggang, Guangxi Autonomous Region. Postal Code: 159073. Phone Number：90315971. E-mail：zigqj@hcywbaen.health.cn

143。姓名: 司空豪珏

住址（湖泊）：广西壮族自治区桂林市恭城瑶族自治县陆盛路 410 号坡彬湖（邮政编码：648916）。联系电话：56195497。电子邮箱：nxzmr@ekcqobmw.lakes.cn

Zhù zhǐ: Sīkōng Háo Jué Guǎngxī Zhuàngzú Zìzhìqū Guìlín Shì Gōng Chéng Yáozú Zìzhìxiàn Lù Chéng Lù 410 Hào Pō Bīn Hú (Yóuzhèng Biānmǎ：648916). Liánxì Diànhuà：56195497. Diànzǐ Yóuxiāng：nxzmr@ekcqobmw.lakes.cn

Hao Jue Sikong, Po Bin Lake, 410 Lu Cheng Road, Gongcheng Yao Autonomous County, Guilin, Guangxi Autonomous Region. Postal Code: 648916. Phone Number：56195497. E-mail：nxzmr@ekcqobmw.lakes.cn

144。姓名: 缑涛福

住址（大学）：广西壮族自治区百色市凌云县自铁大学帆兆路 519 号（邮政编码：174501）。联系电话：44235569。电子邮箱：jcvbg@qlkdavfs.edu.cn

Zhù zhǐ: Gōu Tāo Fú Guǎngxī Zhuàngzú Zìzhìqū Bǎisè Shì Língyún Xiàn Zì Fū DàxuéFān Zhào Lù 519 Hào（Yóuzhèng Biānmǎ：174501). Liánxì Diànhuà：44235569. Diànzǐ Yóuxiāng：jcvbg@qlkdavfs.edu.cn

Tao Fu Gou, Zi Fu University, 519 Fan Zhao Road, Lingyun County, Baise, Guangxi Autonomous Region. Postal Code: 174501. Phone Number：44235569. E-mail：jcvbg@qlkdavfs.edu.cn

145。姓名: 赵帆焯

住址（大学）：广西壮族自治区桂林市恭城瑶族自治县来山大学大科路 187 号（邮政编码：665069）。联系电话：13618593。电子邮箱：xzldm@jbcpfvug.edu.cn

Zhù zhǐ: Zhào Fān Chāo Guǎngxī Zhuàngzú Zìzhìqū Guìlín Shì Gōng Chéng Yáozú Zìzhìxiàn Lái Shān DàxuéDài Kē Lù 187 Hào（Yóuzhèng Biānmǎ：665069). Liánxì Diànhuà：13618593. Diànzǐ Yóuxiāng：xzldm@jbcpfvug.edu.cn

Fan Chao Zhao, Lai Shan University, 187 Dai Ke Road, Gongcheng Yao Autonomous County, Guilin, Guangxi Autonomous Region. Postal Code: 665069. Phone Number：13618593. E-mail：xzldm@jbcpfvug.edu.cn

146。姓名: 宰渊毅

住址（寺庙）：广西壮族自治区崇左市宁明县人浩路 672 号懂红寺（邮政编码：873618）。联系电话：62141534。电子邮箱：rxfbk@kixypcog.god.cn

Zhù zhǐ: Zǎi Yuān Yì Guǎngxī Zhuàngzú Zìzhìqū Chóng Zuǒ Shì Níng Míng Xiàn Rén Hào Lù 672 Hào Dǒng Hóng Sì（Yóuzhèng Biānmǎ：873618). Liánxì Diànhuà：62141534. Diànzǐ Yóuxiāng：rxfbk@kixypcog.god.cn

Yuan Yi Zai, Dong Hong Temple, 672 Ren Hao Road, Ningming County, Chongzuo, Guangxi Autonomous Region. Postal Code: 873618. Phone Number：62141534. E-mail：rxfbk@kixypcog.god.cn

147。姓名: 左丘仲陆

住址（公司）：广西壮族自治区北海市铁山港区骥游路 866 号冠钢有限公司（邮政编码：322988）。联系电话：81833732。电子邮箱：gkzul@qzwvglps.biz.cn

Zhù zhǐ: Zuǒqiū Zhòng Liù Guǎngxī Zhuàngzú Zìzhìqū Běihǎi Shì Tiě Shān Gǎng Qū Jì Yóu Lù 866 Hào Guàn Gāng Yǒuxiàn Gōngsī (Yóuzhèng Biānmǎ：322988). Liánxì Diànhuà：81833732. Diànzǐ Yóuxiāng：gkzul@qzwvglps.biz.cn

Zhong Liu Zuoqiu, Guan Gang Corporation, 866 Ji You Road, Iron Mountain Port District, Beihai, Guangxi Autonomous Region. Postal Code: 322988. Phone Number：81833732. E-mail：gkzul@qzwvglps.biz.cn

148。姓名: 隗葆惟

住址（公共汽车站）：广西壮族自治区梧州市藤县嘉守路 665 号渊化站（邮政编码：479598）。联系电话：19039841。电子邮箱：osntp@eupovlrn.transport.cn

Zhù zhǐ: Kuí Bǎo Wéi Guǎngxī Zhuàngzú Zìzhìqū Wúzhōu Shì Téng Xiàn Jiā Shǒu Lù 665 Hào Yuān Huà Zhàn (Yóuzhèng Biānmǎ：479598). Liánxì Diànhuà：19039841. Diànzǐ Yóuxiāng：osntp@eupovlrn.transport.cn

Bao Wei Kui, Yuan Hua Bus Station, 665 Jia Shou Road, Fuji County, Wuzhou, Guangxi Autonomous Region. Postal Code: 479598. Phone Number：19039841. E-mail：osntp@eupovlrn.transport.cn

149。姓名: 钱胜迅

住址（湖泊）：广西壮族自治区贵港市覃塘区柱葛路 512 号屹刚湖（邮政编码：807766）。联系电话：57469498。电子邮箱：bgjzy@rupvalsb.lakes.cn

Zhù zhǐ: Qián Shēng Xùn Guǎngxī Zhuàngzú Zìzhìqū Guìgǎng Shì Tán Táng Qū Zhù Gé Lù 512 Hào Yì Gāng Hú (Yóuzhèng Biānmǎ：807766). Liánxì Diànhuà：57469498. Diànzǐ Yóuxiāng：bgjzy@rupvalsb.lakes.cn

Sheng Xun Qian, Yi Gang Lake, 512 Zhu Ge Road, Qintang District, Guigang, Guangxi Autonomous Region. Postal Code: 807766. Phone Number：57469498. E-mail：bgjzy@rupvalsb.lakes.cn

150。姓名: 浦水翼

住址（酒店）：广西壮族自治区来宾市武宣县斌刚路 471 号立立酒店（邮政编码：494814）。联系电话：97058680。电子邮箱：nkqai@gkxqzciy.biz.cn

Zhù zhǐ: Pǔ Shuǐ Yì Guǎngxī Zhuàngzú Zìzhìqū Láibīn Shì Wǔxuān Xiàn Bīn Gāng Lù 471 Hào Lì Lì Jiǔ Diàn (Yóuzhèng Biānmǎ：494814). Liánxì Diànhuà：97058680. Diànzǐ Yóuxiāng：nkqai@gkxqzciy.biz.cn

Shui Yi Pu, Li Li Hotel, 471 Bin Gang Road, Wuxuan County, Laibin, Guangxi Autonomous Region. Postal Code: 494814. Phone Number：97058680. E-mail：nkqai@gkxqzciy.biz.cn

Milton Keynes UK
Ingram Content Group UK Ltd.
UKHW030205011223
433552UK00013B/458

9 798887 555218